Santiago de Compostela, Pocket Travel Guide 2023-2024

Explore Santiago de Compostela With Pilgrimage Guide: Discover Day Trips, Insider Travel Tips, Unmissable Festivals 2023-2024, and Enriching Walking Tours"

Alice B. Lowry

1

Table Of Content.

Chapter 3

Language
Common Phrases in Santiago de Compostela
and Their English Translations for Visitors

Chapter 4

Safety
Safety Requirements in Santiago de Compostela,
Ensuring a Secure and Enjoyable Visit.

Chapter 5

Money/Budgeting
Money and Budgeting for a Vacation to Santiago
de Compostela

Chapter 6

Transportation Options in Santiago de
Compostela.

Chapter 7

Arriving in Santiago de Compostela.
Arriving in Santiago de Compostela, Exploring Friendly Neighborhoods and Navigating from the Airport

Chapter 8

The Rules.
Detailed Instructions on Santiago de Compostela Laws and Etiquette for Visitors.

Chapter 9

Accommodation Options and Suitable Budget in Santiago de Compostela.
Homestays
Rentals
Hotels

Chapter 10

Best Time to Visit Santiago de Compostela Greece, Embrace the Perfect Weather Conditions.

Chapter 11

Santiago de Compostela's Top Tourist Destinations You Must See and Booking Tips.

- *Santiago de Compostela Cathedral: A Guide to a Memorable Visit*

- *Plaza Quintana: Unveiling the Charm of Santiago de Compostela*

- *Parque de la Alameda: Santiago's Green Oasis.*

- *Mercado de Abastos de Santiago: A Culinary Adventure in Galicia*

- *Praza das Praterías: Where History and Beauty Converge*

- *Parque de la Alameda: Santiago's Scenic Oasis.*

Bonus

Santiago de Compostela's Scenic Sit-Out Points: A Haven for Recreation

Chapter 15

Souvenir Shopping
Souvenir Shopping in *Santiago de Compostela*, Discovering Authentic Mementos of the Eternal City.

Chapter 16

A Dream Vacation in Santiago de Compostela: A 14-Day Itinerary.
Tips
Tips and Essential Information for Travelers Visiting Santiago de Compostela.

Introduction

From Wanderer to Author: William's Journey to Santiago de Compostela"

William has always had a restless spirit and a deep desire to explore new places. Despite his extensive travels, he had never managed to reach Santiago de Compostela, the holy city situated at the conclusion of the Camino de Santiago pilgrimage route.

As William sipped his coffee in a quaint Lisbon café one crisp autumn morning, he found himself flipping through a travel guidebook on Santiago de Compostela. The book described the spiritual value that attracted pilgrims from all walks of life, as well as the fascinating journey along the Camino and the city's rich history. It created a striking image of verdant landscapes, majestic cathedrals, and cobblestone streets.

Something inside William was sparked by the handbook. Though he had read a great deal about the Camino de Santiago and Santiago de Compostela, something felt off. Like a calling, it seemed. He made the decision to go on this pilgrimage in order to share his experiences with others in addition to doing it for himself.

William began preparing for his expedition with indomitable will. He looked into the ideal time to walk the Camino, necessary equipment, and various walking routes. He made connections with other pilgrims who had similar dreams and asked more experienced pilgrims for assistance. His compact Lisbon flat turned into a hive of activity, with walking shoes, guidebooks, and maps all over the living room.

William finally got to pack his rucksack, lace up his boots, and start the first part of his Camino expedition on this day. The first few steps were thrilling, full of wonder and anticipation. He encountered pilgrims on route from all over the world, each with their own backstories and motivations for setting out on this spiritual quest.

William felt a strong connection to Galicia's history and nature as he strolled through charming villages, across undulating vineyards, and across historic bridges. He was awestruck by the pilgrims' friendship, the shared meals at the quaint albergues, and the starry nights spent sharing stories of the day's exploits.

Eventually, after travelling for weeks, William reached Santiago de Compostela. He gasped at seeing the magnificent Santiago Cathedral. He went to the Pilgrim's Mass, where the hallowed space was filled with symbolism and incense by the swinging Botafumeiro. William was overcome with a feeling of achievement and spiritual contentment, indicating that he had discovered his purpose.

After arriving back in Lisbon, William was consumed with the desire to tell others about his adventure. He believed that there was a need for a travel handbook that captured the spirit of the Camino experience, including the friendships made, the vistas experienced, and the personal changes experienced, in addition to providing useful information.

William put his heart and effort into creating a guidebook unlike any other, drawing from his personal experiences. The book "Explore Santiago de Compostela with Travel Preparation Guide: The Camino de Santiago Experience" entered into publication. Not only did he include recommendations and directions in this handbook, but he also gave personal tales, wonderful photos of the landscapes, and insightful commentary on the pilgrim's way of thinking.

William's handbook became well-known among both tourists and pilgrims very fast. His narrative struck a chord with readers, encouraging them to set out on their own adventures. In addition to offering helpful tips on what to bring, where to stay, and what to anticipate on the Camino, he urged readers to welcome the pilgrimage's spiritual and life-changing elements.

In addition to satisfying William's desire to travel, his trip to Santiago de Compostela sparked a desire in him to spread the wonder of the Camino to as many people as possible. He persisted in writing, exploring new places, and inspiring others, demonstrating that occasionally a trip may result in more than just a final destination—it can also produce something lovely and significant that others would treasure.

Santiago de Compostela: A Timeless Gem of Spain

Spain's essence is embodied in the city of Santiago de Compostela, sometimes just called Santiago. Santiago is a city in northwest Spain's lush Galicia area where spirituality, culture, and history all come together in a fascinating way. With a rich and varied history dating back more than a millennium, Santiago de Compostela is a city well-known around the world as the culmination point of the Camino de Santiago pilgrimage. We shall delve into the many fascinating aspects of Santiago de Compostela in this extensive review, covering everything from its spiritual significance and historical roots to its vibrant current life and cultural treasures.

Part 1: Historical Background

1.1 Saint James's Legend:

The history of Santiago de Compostela is closely associated with the mythological character of

Saint James, also known as Santiago in Spanish, who was one of Jesus Christ's twelve disciples. According to legend, Saint James traveled to the Iberian Peninsula as a missionary and preached Christianity there.

In 1.2 The Tomb of Saint James Found:

In the ninth century, a hermit by the name of Pelayo claimed to have seen celestial lights that guided him to the location of Saint James' tomb, which is how the city's history began. The religious significance of Santiago began with this amazing incident.

Section 2: The Camino de Santiago's Spiritual Center

2.1 The Santiago Camino:

One of the most well-known pilgrimage routes in the world, the Camino de Santiago (also known as the Way of Saint James), ends at Santiago de Compostela. For centuries, pilgrims from all over the world have been trekking hundreds of kilometers to visit the city and honor Saint James as part of this spiritual trip.

2.2 The Cathedral of Santiago:

Situated at the heart of the city's spiritual character is the centuries-old architectural masterpiece known as the Santiago Cathedral. The city's unwavering faith is demonstrated by its breathtaking fusion of Romanesque, Gothic, Baroque, and Renaissance architectural styles.

3.3.2 Mass for Pilgrims and Botafumeiro:

The Pilgrim's Mass at the cathedral is one of Santiago's most treasured customs. At this unique ritual, pilgrims congregate to commemorate their journey and get blessings. The giant incense burner known as the Botafumeiro, which swings through the transept of the cathedral and fills the air with beautiful aroma, is a highlight of the mass.

Section 3: Magnificent Buildings

Old Town (3.1):

The Old Town of Santiago de Compostela, a maze of squares and streets made of cobblestone, is recognized as a UNESCO World Heritage site. Numerous architectural gems, including as old churches, monasteries, and palaces, can be found there.

3.2.1 The Obradoiro Plaza:

Santiago's biggest square, Praza do Obradoiro, provides a stunning perspective of the façade of the Santiago Cathedral. Important structures surround it, such as the Hostal dos Reis Católicos, an opulent parador that was formerly a pilgrims' hospital.

3.3 The Architecture of Galicia Like Nothing Else:

Santiago is a great example of traditional Galician architecture, with its stone facades, quaint wooden balconies, and elaborate ironwork. The city's old structures serve as a reminder of the distinctive architectural style of the area.

Section 4: Customs and Cultural Heritage

4.1 Culture of Galicia:

Within Spain, Santiago de Compostela is a bastion of Galician culture, a unique and proud regional identity. The entire city celebrates the Galician language, music, dancing, and culinary traditions.

4.2 Holidays and Festivities:

All year long, Santiago is the site of several festivals and cultural events. The colorful San Froilán Festival in October and the Feast of Saint James on July 25th are two notable festivals.

Section 5: Santiago of Today

5.1 A City of Universities:

The University of Santiago de Compostela, one of Spain's most esteemed academic institutions, is located in Santiago. Its presence gives the city a lively intellectual atmosphere and a youthful vitality.

5.2 Gastronomy and Cuisine:

Modern gastronomy and traditional Galician flavors are combined in Santiago's food scene. Visit the neighborhood bars and eateries to sample local specialties like empanadas and pulpo a la gallega (octopus).

5.3 Culture and Art:

The city is home to a large number of theaters, art galleries, and other cultural venues that present both regional and global talent. Santiago's vibrant cultural landscape is bolstered by a strong artistic community.

Section 6: Present-Day Santiago de Compostela

6.1 Travel & Voyage:

Both tourists and pilgrims from all over the world continue to come to Santiago de Compostela. For many, the Camino de Santiago is still a very spiritual journey; for others, it is an opportunity to engage with culture.

6.2 Recognition of UNESCO World Heritage:

The city's UNESCO World Heritage designation emphasizes its historical and cultural significance. By preserving its architectural and cultural assets, Santiago makes sure that future generations can enjoy them.

6.3 A Resilient City:

Throughout its history, Santiago de Compostela has triumphed against both setbacks and victories, including invasions and restorations. Visitors are consistently enthralled and inspired by this city because of its resiliency and enduring character.

An Ageless Jewel

With its fascinating past, deep spiritual significance, amazing architecture, and lively cultural scene, Santiago de Compostela is a city that stands the test of time. It's a location where the past and present live in harmony, fostering an environment that encourages discovery, reflection, and celebration. Travelers seeking cultural enrichment or pilgrims seeking spiritual enlightenment will find Santiago de Compostela to be a memorable excursion into Spain's heart and soul. All who are lured to its legendary streets and the everlasting legend of Saint James are beckoned by this ageless gem.

Brief History Of Santiago de Compostela: A Journey Through History.

Nestled in the lush hills of northwest Spain, Santiago de Compostela is a city whose history is as varied and rich as the pilgrims who have been there through the years. Santiago, which is the last stop on the Camino de Santiago pilgrimage route, has been a hub for study, culture, and religion since its founding in the ninth century. This essay will take us on a historical tour of the fascinating history of Santiago de Compostela, from its fabled beginnings to its current position as a revered pilgrimage and spirituality icon and UNESCO World Heritage site.

Section 1: Mythical Beginnings

1.1 Saint James's Legend:

The legend of Saint James, or Santiago in Spanish, opens the history of Santiago de Compostela. James was one of Jesus' twelve apostles, and Christian legend states that he went to the Iberian Peninsula to preach Christianity. He was crucified upon his return to Jerusalem, and legend has it that his remains were magically returned to Galicia, Spain.

1.2 Finding the Tomb:

A hermit by the name of Pelayo claimed to have seen a sequence of supernatural lights that guided him to the location of Saint James's tomb around the beginning of the ninth century. The prominence of Santiago de Compostela in religion began with the finding of the saint's remains.

Section 2: Ascending as a Site of Pilgrimage

2.1 Building of the Cathedral of Santiago:

On the spot where Saint James's remains were thought to be interred, a magnificent church was built as a memorial to him. The Santiago Cathedral was built over several decades, starting in 1075. It is a masterwork of architecture, showcasing a striking blend of

Gothic, Baroque, Renaissance, and Romanesque architectural styles.

2.2 The Santiago Camino:

The Camino de Santiago, often known as the Way of Saint James, emerged around the same time as the cathedral was being built. Traveling to Santiago de Compostela, pilgrims from all across Europe came to honor Saint James. The city's identity was shaped by the Camino de Santiago, which developed into a spiritual and cultural phenomenon.

Section 3: The Cultural Center of Santiago de Compostela

3.1 Intellectual and Educational Center:

During the Middle Ages, Santiago de Compostela developed into a major hub of scholarship and culture. Since its founding in 1495, the city's university has drawn academics from all around Europe. The first books printed in Spain were released from this location.

3.2 The Language and Culture of Galicia:

In order to preserve and advance Galician language and culture, the city was essential. One of Spain's official regional tongues is Galician, and Galician customs—such as music, literature, and festivals—remain strong in Santiago de Compostela.

Section 4: Difficult Times and Resurrection

4.1 The Invasion of France:

During the Napoleonic Wars, Santiago de Compostela experienced unrest in the early 19th century. The church was looted during the French invasion, and the city went through hard times.

4.2 The 20th Century's Revival:

In the 20th century, Santiago de Compostela had a renaissance. An attempt was made to preserve the cathedral's cultural legacy and rehabilitate it. The city received the UNESCO World Heritage designation in 1985.

Section 5: Santiago in the Present: A Sign of Spirituality and Pilgrimage

5.1 Contemporary Journey:

Travelers from all over the world continue to be drawn to Santiago de Compostela. One of the most well-known pilgrimage paths in the world, the Camino de Santiago draws pilgrims who are seeking spiritual, cultural, or personal experiences from both religious and nonreligious sources.

5.2 Treasures of Culture and Art:

The Santiago Cathedral is still a major attraction in the city because of its magnificent architecture and spiritual significance. During the Pilgrim's Mass, a noteworthy sight is the cathedral's enormous incense burner, known as the Botafumeiro.

Approved as a UNESCO World Heritage Site:

The Old Town of Santiago de Compostela was honored with UNESCO World Heritage status in

1985, a testament to its historical and cultural value. The city's historic center is a superb example of its illustrious history.

Section 6: Concluding Remarks: An Eternal Journey

The history of Santiago de Compostela is a wonderful trip through time, from its fabled origins based in the life of Saint James to its current standing as a spiritual and pilgrimage center. The city has faced difficulties, welcomed cultural variety, and developed into a center of scholarship and culture over the ages.

Inviting pilgrims and tourists from all walks of life to set off on a voyage of self-discovery and exploration, Santiago de Compostela greets them today. Trekking the Camino de Santiago is still a popular choice for people looking for adventure, introspection, or a closer spiritual connection because of its rich traditions and beautiful scenery.

If we look back at the history of the city, we can see that Santiago de Compostela is a place where history, faith, and culture come together in a way that is truly unique and transformative. This is because the city's charm is not only derived from its breathtaking architecture but also from the everlasting legacy of Saint James and the timeless spirit of pilgrimage.

Chapter 1

Planning Your Memorable Trip to Santiago de Compostela: A Comprehensive Guide

A must-see location in the center of Galicia, Spain, is Santiago de Compostela, a city with a rich historical background, breathtaking architecture, and spiritual significance. Organizing a vacation to Santiago de Compostela is an exciting undertaking, regardless of whether you're a pilgrim traveling the Camino de Santiago or a tourist looking to experience a different culture. We will go over all you need to know in this extensive guide, including what to expect, how to get around, and a list of things you simply must do while in the city.

Important Paperwork and Visa Requirements:

Make sure you have all the required paperwork in order before starting your trip to Santiago de Compostela:

Make sure your passport is valid for a minimum of six months after the day you intend to depart.

Visa: Since Spain is a member of the Schengen Area, many visitors from a number of nations are exempt from the need for a visa for visits that are typically no longer than 90 days. But always be sure to find out well in advance of your trip what kind of visa is required for your country of residence.

Pilgrimage Credential: Obtain a pilgrim's credential (Credencial del Peregrino) at the beginning of your journey or from your local pilgrim association if you're walking the Camino de Santiago. If you plan to stay in pilgrim hostels along the route, you will need this passport.

2. Best Time to Travel to Santiago de Compostela:

Because of Santiago's variable climate, it's crucial to plan your visit whilst there. Here are some things to think about:

Summer, which runs from June to August, is the busiest travel season due to the often warm and pleasant weather. Aim for greater prices and larger crowds.

The shoulder seasons of spring (March to May) and autumn (September to November) provide more agreeable travel conditions, less crowds, and milder temperatures.

Winter (December to February): Santiago's Christmas traditions are charming, even if the weather might be chilly and wet. It is a unique time to visit if you don't mind the chill.

Steps for traveling to Santiago de Compostela:

Via Air:

The primary airport in the area, Santiago Airport (SCQ), has excellent connections to important cities in Spain and Europe. To get to the city core, take a quick cab or bus ride from the airport.

Via Rail:

RENFE: Trains to Santiago are run by Spain's national railway operator, RENFE, from places including Madrid, Barcelona, and Porto (Portugal). Estación de Santiago de Compostela, the train station, is conveniently situated.

Via Bus:

Bus trips: From a number of Spanish cities, ALSA and FlixBus are two bus companies that provide reasonably priced interstate bus trips to Santiago.

4. Transport Within the Urban Area:

Because Santiago de Compostela is a small city, walking around is a breeze. There are, though, additional practical modes of transportation:

Walking: Exploring the city's charms on foot is the most recommended activity. Within the ancient Old Town lies the majority of the main attractions.

Public Transportation: Tickets can be bought at kiosks or on the buses themselves. Santiago has an effective bus system. Taxis are also easily accessible, albeit a little more costly.

Cycles: The city offers a pleasant and environmentally responsible method to get around called "Bicicoruña," which is a bike-sharing program.

5. Lodging Selections:

A variety of lodging choices are available in Santiago de Compostela to accommodate a range of spending limits and tastes:

Hostels for travelers (Albergues): If you're walking the Camino de Santiago, these are reasonably priced lodgings designed with travelers in mind. Though simple, they provide a distinctive community experience.

Hotels: There is a wide range of hotels in Santiago, from opulent properties to reasonably priced choices. If you want to be close to the sights, staying in the historic Old Town is a popular alternative.

Bed & Breakfasts and guesthouses: These offer a more individualized experience and frequently have quaint, regionally inspired décor.

Vacation Rentals & Apartments: If you're planning a longer stay or traveling with a larger party, renting an apartment will let you explore Santiago like a local.

6. Must Visit Points:

There are so many historical and cultural riches in Santiago de Compostela. Here are a few standouts:

The magnificent Santiago Cathedral, also known as the Cathedral de Santiago, is the pilgrims' final stop on the Camino de Santiago. It is located in the center of the city. Come to the Pilgrim's Mass and see the magnificent incense swinging Botafumeiro.

Plaza del Obradoiro: A great site to begin your research is the large area in front of the cathedral. Admire the stunning architecture and take in the lively ambiance.

Parque Alameda: A calm urban park with statues and fountains that provides a break from the bustle of the city.

The educational museum, Museo das Peregrinaciones e de Santiago, offers information on the cultural relevance and historical background of the Camino de Santiago pilgrimage.

Monasterio de San Martín Pinario: An amazing monastery featuring a Baroque façade that provides guided tours illuminating its extensive past.

Santiago's thriving food market, Praza de Abastos, is a great place to try delicious Galician cuisine and fresh products.

Colexio de San Xerome: Take a tour of this stunning 16th-century building's library, which is filled with priceless manuscripts and elaborate woodwork.

7. Examining the Cuisine of Galicia:

Santiago de Compostela is a paradise for food lovers. Don't pass up the chance to enjoy these delicious Galician foods:

Pulpo a la Gallega: octopus prepared in the Galician style, usually served with olive oil and paprika.

Empanadas are savory pastries stuffed with a range of ingredients, such as vegetables, seafood, or meat.

Tarta de Santiago: A sweet almond cake with the cross of Saint James and powdered sugar on top.

Have a taste of the crisp and delightful Albariño wine, which is the native white wine.

fish: Galicia has an abundance of fresh fish due to its closeness to the shore. Taste foods like mariscada, a seafood mix, and percebes, which are goose barnacles.

Queimada: Aguardiente, sugar, and coffee beans are the main ingredients of this traditional Galician alcoholic beverage, which is frequently ceremoniously produced with a flaming sugar cube.

Local customs and cultural etiquette:

To guarantee a courteous and pleasurable vacation to Santiago de Compostela, it is unquestionably imperative to comprehend local customs and cultural etiquette. The following significant cultural conventions and practices should be remembered:

Salutations: In general, Spaniards are kind and amiable. Among friends and acquaintances, a kiss on both cheeks is the customary welcome. It is customary to shake hands in more formal situations. Unless specifically asked to use their first name, address someone by their title (Mr., Mrs., or Dr.) followed by their last name.

Spanish people typically take a more casual attitude toward timeliness. Although punctuality is crucial for appointments, allow an extra few minutes for flexibility at social events.

Mealtime Etiquette: Spanish society places a lot of emphasis on dining, and there are some traditions to follow when dining:

Prior to starting to eat, wait for the host to start the meal.

Keep your elbows off the table; keep your hands there instead.

Taking care of everything on your plate is courteous.

Make sure to bring a small gift, such as wine, chocolates, or flowers, if you are asked to someone's house.

Tipping: It is traditional in cafes, restaurants, and pubs to leave a tip. Tipping is customary in Spain and usually consists of rounding up the price or leaving a 10% tip.

Although Santiago de Compostela is a laid-back city, modest clothing is required when visiting places of worship, such as the cathedral. Keep your shoulders covered and stay away from anything too exposing. Most of the time, casual clothing is appropriate.

Language: Although many people in the region speak English, especially in tourist regions, speaking Spanish or Galician, the regional dialect, is appreciated. Gaining some basic language proficiency will greatly improve your experience.

Siesta: As was already noted, many places of business observe the customary siesta, which is observed for a few hours in the afternoon. Remember that this is a time for rest and relaxation, so keep the noise level down.

Religious Respect: There are significant religious relationships in Santiago de Compostela. Exhibit a courteous attitude when entering places of worship. Put your phone on silent and refrain from being disruptive when attending religious ceremonies.

Local Festivals: Take part in the celebrations and honor the customs if you happen to visit during a local holiday or celebration. Processions, singing, and dancing are possible at certain festivals.

Salutations on the Camino: "Buen Camino!" is the standard greeting among pilgrims who are walking the Camino de Santiago. This is a polite way of wishing other travelers well on their travels.

Local Markets: Be ready to haggle, especially for artisanal goods, and interact politely with vendors as you shop at local markets like the Mercado de Abastos.

Tolerance: Spain is renowned for being tolerant and open-minded. In general, LGBTQ+ visitors ought to feel at ease in Santiago de Compostela.

You'll not only have a better time in Santiago de Compostela if you are aware of and respectful of these cultural norms and conventions, but you'll also make a good impression on the people you meet along the way. Respecting regional traditions and customs is a great approach to get to know this lovely city's people and culture.

Packing Tips for Santiago de Compostela.

When planning your luggage for a vacation to Santiago de Compostela, take into account the weather, outdoor activities, and cultural offerings of the city. Below is a detailed inventory of everything you'll need to make your visit pleasant and enjoyable:

Comfortable Walking Shoes: If you intend to explore the surrounding countryside or walk a portion of the Camino, you will need comfortable walking shoes or hiking boots due to Santiago's cobblestone streets and rugged terrain.

Dress appropriately for the weather: Galicia's weather is notoriously erratic. Bring multiple layers, such as an umbrella or waterproof jacket, because rain is a year-round occurrence. Winter wears heavier clothing, while summer wears light, breathable clothing.

bag: Useful for transporting necessities like water, food, and a camera when touring the city and its environs, a robust bag will keep you organized.

Travel adapters: Santiago is equipped with regular European power outlets, so bring along the essential travel adapters and gadget chargers.

Carry a reusable water bottle so you can fill it up at any of the many public fountains in the city and stay hydrated on your activities.

A paper guidebook or map can be quite helpful for navigating the Old Town's winding streets and locating areas of interest, even though smartphone apps are convenient.

trip Documents: Make sure you have your airline tickets, passport, visa (if needed), trip insurance, and any other documents that may be needed.

Essentials for Money and Banking: Have a credit or debit card with you and bring some cash in euros. To avoid card problems overseas, let your bank know about your travel schedule.

Medicines and First Aid Supplies: Bring along any essential drugs and a basic first aid pack that includes bandages, analgesics, and stomach medication.

Toiletries: Although Santiago has stores that sell toiletries, it's a good idea to pack the necessities, such as shampoo, soap, toothbrush, and a small towel.

Travel Locks: Use travel locks to fasten your bag and luggage to protect your possessions.

Travel eye mask and pillow: These devices might improve your quality of sleep and comfort during extended travels.

Travel Insurance: It's a good idea to get coverage for unanticipated circumstances such as trip cancellations, medical emergencies, and other catastrophes.

Bring a camera and binoculars to capture moments and discover wildlife. Santiago and its surrounds offer plenty of beautiful chances.

Snacks: Bring along some energy bars or almonds to keep you going as you explore.

Let's now examine a few of the distinctive products Santiago de Compostela has to offer:

Recommended Things to Purchase in Santiago de Compostela:

Pilgrim's Scallop Shell: The Camino de Santiago is often recognized by the scallop shell. Several stores sell exquisitely made shells as mementos.

Local Ceramics: The elaborate ceramics of Galicia are well-known. To find one-of-a-kind presents or mementos, look for handcrafted ceramics, such as plates, bowls, and ornamental pieces.

Traditional Galician Textiles: Well-known traditional fabrics from Galicia include linen and lace. Tablecloths, napkins, and apparel constructed of these materials are available for purchase.

Wines from Galicia: The region of Rías Baixas is known for its superb Albariño wine. Shop for wine locally and bring home a bottle or two.

Saffron: Galician saffron, sometimes referred to as "azafrán," is of excellent quality and gives your food a distinct flavor. Check your neighborhood markets or specialty food stores for saffron.

Local Cheeses: Tetilla and San Simón are two of the many varieties of cheese available in Galicia. These cheeses are great as picnic fare or as delightful mementos.

Galician Craft Beer: In Galicia, craft beer is growing in popularity. Visit nearby breweries and sample some interesting beers to bring home.

Authentic Galician dishes: Get authentic Galician dishes like chorizo, empanadas, and artisanal honey at markets like Mercado de Abastos.

Handcrafted Jewelry: Santiago is home to gifted jewelers who produce one-of-a-kind items. As a unique memento, think about purchasing a handcrafted piece of gold or silver.

Celtic and Camino Jewelry: To mark your visit, choose jewelry based on Celtic and Camino symbols, such as the Camino shell or Celtic knots.

Instruments of Traditional Music: Galicia is well-known for its traditional music, and local shops often stock instruments like tambourines and bagpipes.

Books & Literature: There are numerous bookshops in Santiago de Compostela that sell literature pertaining to the Camino and Galician cultures.

Cultural Artifacts: Look through antique stores to find one-of-a-kind historical objects, religious relics, or vintage postcards.

Handwoven Baskets: Traditionally constructed from chestnut branches, Galician baskets are lovely and useful mementos.

Religious art and candles: Santiago has a rich religious past. As mementos of your stay, you can find religious candles, statues, and artwork.

There are many things to buy in Santiago de Compostela, from gastronomic treats to cultural mementos. If souvenirs, presents, or locally made goods are what you're looking for, you'll have no trouble finding what you want when you come.

Chapter 2

Visa and Entry Requirements for Santiago de Compostela.

As the last stop on the Camino de Santiago pilgrimage, Santiago de Compostela, which is located in the picturesque Galicia region of northwest Spain, has long enthralled tourists with its fascinating history, breathtaking architecture, and spiritual significance. But, it's important to comprehend the visa application procedure, customs advice, and entry and visa criteria before you set out on your trip to this fascinating city. This thorough guide will lead you through every step, guaranteeing a hassle-free and easy trip to Santiago de Compostela.

Entry and Visa Requirements

1. Assess Your Need for a Visa:

Finding out if you require a visa in order to enter Spain is the first step in organizing your trip to Santiago de Compostela. Because Spain is a member of the Schengen Area, travel between its member nations is permitted without a passport. Certain nationals of certain nations are exempt from needing a visa for quick trips (up to 90 days) inside the Schengen Area for business or tourism. These nations comprise the majority of the European Union's member states as well as the US, Canada, and Australia. Nevertheless, laws might change, so it's critical to confirm the most recent specifications unique to your country of origin.

2. Types of Visa:

In the event that you do need a visa, you must apply for the right kind. When visiting Santiago de Compostela, the most popular visa categories for visitors are:

With a tourist visa, also known as a Schengen visa, you are able to travel to Spain to see friends and family. Usually, it is good for ninety days out of a total of 180 days.

Business Visa: You might require a business visa if you're traveling for work-related activities like attending conferences or meetings.

Visa requirements for pilgrimages: There can be specific visa categories or paperwork needed for individuals starting the Camino de Santiago pilgrimage. For detailed information, it is best to contact the Spanish consulate or embassy in your nation.

3. Applying for a Visa:

This is a step-by-step guide to applying for a Santiago de Compostela visa:

a. Choose Where to Apply: Research the Spanish consulate or embassy that deals with visa applications in your nation. Applications may occasionally be accepted by consulates in nearby nations.

a. Gather Required Documents: Get ready the required paperwork, which usually consists of the following: - A filled-out visa application form. - A passport that is up to date, has two blank pages, and is valid for at least three months after the day you want to depart. - Current passport-sized pictures that adhere to Spanish requirements. - Documentation of travel plans, like airline tickets. - Travel insurance that pays for medical costs up to 30,000 euros. - Proof of accommodation in Santiago de Compostela. - Bank statements or other records attesting to your ability to pay for your stay. - A cover letter outlining your itinerary and the reason for your visit. - Receipt for payment of visa application fee.

c. Make an Appointment: In order to submit your visa application, many Spanish consulates and embassies ask you to make an appointment. Please refer to the consulate's website for detailed guidelines on making meetings.

d. Show Up for the Visa Interview: Show up at the consulate or embassy for the planned visa interview. Be ready to provide biometric information (fingerprints, for example), respond to inquiries regarding your journey, and turn in your paperwork.

e. Pay the Visa Fee: Depending on your country and the type of visa you need, you must pay a non-refundable application fee. Make sure you pay the fee the way the embassy instructs you to.

f. Wait for Processing: It's best to apply for a visa well in advance of the day you intend to travel, though processing times can vary. The time frame for processing can range from a few weeks to many months.

g. Pick Up Your Visa: If your application is accepted, pick it up from the embassy or consulate. Examine the entrance requirements and validity dates of the visa thoroughly.

4. Procedures for Customs and Entry:

Following the acquisition of your visa and your arrival in Santiago de Compostela, you must be aware of the following customs and entry requirements:

Passport Control: You will have to go through passport control when you arrive in Spain. Show the immigration officer your passport, visa, and any supporting documentation they may ask for. If your sort of visa requires it, make sure your passport is stamped.

Custom Declarations: Know what you are and are not allowed to carry into Spain. Learn about the rules governing import limitations, alcohol, tobacco, and other things that are subject to customs laws.

Suggestions from Customs: In order to facilitate your entry and guarantee a seamless customs experience, take into account the following advice:

Declare anything you carry: To avoid fines, notify customs officials of any products you are carrying that must be declared, such as pricey electronics or sizable sums of cash.

Save receipts: Save the receipts for any purchases you make overseas. A proof of purchase value may be requested by customs officials.

Be aware of duty-free limits: Recognize what products, such as alcohol and tobacco, are allowed to be purchased duty-free. If these thresholds are exceeded, taxes and customs charges may apply.

Look for banned items: Become familiar with the things that aren't allowed into Spain, like some products made from plants or animals or drugs.

Declare pharmaceuticals: If you are carrying prescription drugs, ensure they are in their original packaging and have your name clearly written on them. Keep a copy of the prescription with you, particularly if it contains any restricted medications.

Health and Safety: Be current on health and safety regulations, particularly in view of any lingering worries about the state of the world's health. Make sure you fulfill any health-related prerequisites for entrance, such as COVID-19 testing or certifications of vaccination.

Respect Local Laws and Customs: To guarantee a courteous and culturally aware stay, familiarize yourself with Spain's legal system and customs. For instance, it is against the law to smoke in indoor public areas, and it is important to observe any clothing requirements that may apply, particularly while visiting places of worship.

Language: Although English is widely spoken in Santiago de Compostela, knowing a few basic Spanish phrases will improve your experience and make communication with locals simpler in a variety of settings.

Traveling to Santiago de Compostela is an exploration, spiritual, and cultural experience. To guarantee a smooth and pleasurable vacation, it is essential to comprehend the visa and entry needs, customs advice, and the visa application procedure. Following the rules will allow you to fully enjoy the city's breathtaking architecture, lively culture, and rich history while making the most of your trip to this alluring location in Galicia, Spain.

Planning Your Unforgettable Trip to Santiago de Compostela, Dos, Don'ts, and Essential Tips.

The experience of organizing a journey to Santiago de Compostela may be life-changing. To make the most of your trip, whether you're traveling on the well-known Camino de Santiago pilgrimage or just visiting the city to see its extensive history and culture, you need to be well-prepared with a list of dos and don'ts. We will go over the essential information that all first-time visitors to Santiago de Compostela should be aware of in this extensive guide.

Situated in the Galician region of northwest Spain, Santiago de Compostela is a deeply spiritual, culturally rich, and historically significant city. It is well known for being the last stop on the Camino de Santiago, one of the most well-known pilgrimage routes in the world, which draws thousands of travelers and pilgrims each year. The Santiago de Compostela

Cathedral, an architectural wonder and a representation of devotion, lies at the center of the city.

Action Items for New Visitors:

Investigate the Old Town:

Do: Take a tour of Santiago's ancient Old Town to start your adventure. Explore its winding, small streets and take in the enchanting squares, lanes, and quaint buildings.

Go to the Cathedral of Santiago de Compostela:

Do: The most recognizable landmark in the city is the Santiago de Compostela Cathedral. See the Pilgrim's Mass, but if you can, go when it's less crowded to truly experience the peace and serenity of the site.

Sample Food from the Area:

Do: Savour the traditional Galician fare, including fresh fish, empanadas (savory pastries), and "pulpo a la gallega" (octopus). Serve your meals with a refreshing Estrella Galicia beer or a local Albariño wine.

Take Part in the Pilgrimage:

Do: Get fully immersed in the pilgrim experience, even if you aren't walking the Camino de Santiago. Take in the pilgrim's Mass, watch the big incense burner, or botafumeiro, swing, and converse with pilgrims to learn about their experiences.

Take Up Spanish:

Do: Although English is widely spoken among the locals, knowing a few simple Spanish words will improve your interactions with non-native speakers and make your trip more enjoyable.

Travel for a Day:

Do: Magnificent rural scenery envelops Santiago. Think of going on a day excursion to one of the surrounding seaside villages, Finisterre, or exploring Galicia's magnificent countryside.

Observe regional customs:

Do: The rituals and schedules of Spanish culture are unique. A lot of stores close in the afternoon, so be ready for a nap. Dinner is usually served late, usually after 9 PM.

First-Time Visitor Don'ts:

Don't Hasten Your Journey:

Don't: Refrain from rushing the Camino de Santiago if you're walking it. Reaching the destination is not the main focus; the experience is. Savor each moment as you go along, and take your time.

Don't Wear Unsuitable Clothes:

Don't: Wear modest clothing when you visit places of worship like the cathedral. Respect the holy area by avoiding skimpy attire and making sure your knees and shoulders are covered.

Remember the Siesta Hours:

Don't forget: Many establishments close during siesta hours, which typically begin at 2:00 PM and last at 5:00 PM. Plan out what you're going to do.

Keep an Eye on Local Festivals:

Don't: Throughout the year, Santiago de Compostela holds a number of festivals. If there are any celebrations scheduled for the time you are visiting, check the local calendar. A wonderful opportunity to get a taste of the local way of life.

Never Give Too Much Tipping:

Don't: Unlike in several other nations, tipping is not customary in Spain. Although greatly appreciated, leaving a large gratuity is not customary. Tipping a little or rounding up the amount is adequate.

Don't Go Expecting a Quick Lifestyle:

Don't: The laid-back lifestyle of Santiago de Compostela is well-known. Things move slowly, especially when you're eating. Savor the relaxed ambiance.

Remember to Drink Plenty of Water:

Don't: It rains a lot and the weather in Galicia is erratic. Keep yourself hydrated and carry an umbrella or raincoat, particularly if you plan on walking a lot.

Extra Advice for a Trip You Won't Soon Forget:

Accommodations: Reserve your lodging well in advance, particularly if you intend to travel during the busiest times for pilgrimages. For a truly unique experience, think about booking a stay in a typical Galician "pazo" (manor house).

Even though Santiago is a walking city, you should think about taking the public transit or renting a bike to explore the surroundings.

Safety: While Santiago is a fairly safe city, like with any other, keep an eye out for your possessions, especially in crowded locations.

Local Markets: Take in the sights, sounds, and flavors of regional products and cuisine by visiting the Mercado de Abastos, the city's busy food market.

Language: Galician, a regional language, is also spoken, while Spanish is the official language. When tourists attempt to speak simple Spanish phrases, the locals find it rather appreciative.

Visit Santiago's galleries and museums, like the Centro Galego de Arte Contemporánea and the

Museo de las Peregrinaciones, to learn more about the city's contemporary art and culture.

Savor the Nightlife: Santiago's thriving nightlife culture makes the city come to life at night. Discover the city's tapas bars and take in live music at one of the various places.

Regardless of your personal beliefs, you should treat religious sites with respect when you visit them. Please turn off your phone and act with civility.

The distinctive fusion of history, faith, and culture that Santiago de Compostela offers can make your vacation absolutely unforgettable. You'll be ready to go on an informative and enjoyable trip to this quaint Spanish city if you heed these dos and don'ts and take into account the extra advice.

Chapter 3

Language
Common Phrases in Santiago de Compostela and Their English Translations for Visitors.

Speaking both Spanish and Galician, Santiago de Compostela is a multilingual city. Although Spanish (Castilian) is the official language of Spain, many Galicians are proud of their cultural background and still speak Galician in daily conversation. Galician is the regional language. While it's usual to hear English spoken in tourist regions, it might be courteous to know a few simple words in the local tongue and enhance the quality of your conversations.

Simple Salutations and Etiquette

Hello, or Hola

In English: Hi

Salutations - Good morning.

In English: Good day.

Felices tardes - Good evening/afternoon.

In English: Good day or night.

Noches buenas - Good evening

In English: Good evening.

En que estás? How do you feel?

Hey, how are you in English?

I'm grateful; thank you

English: Regards

Forgive me, please

Please in English

De nada - Thank you very much

English: Thank you very much

Requesting Directions

"Where are you..." -Where is that?

English: Where's that?

El establecimiento municipal - The city center

Eng: The heart of the city

The cathedral, or la catedral

In English: The church

La estación de tren/bus - The station for trains and buses

English: The bus/train terminal

How long does it take to get to...? - How much time does it take to arrive at...?

English: What's the approximate travel time to...?

¿Está allá? Is that far?

English: How far is it?

To the right, or to the left

Language: To the right

On the left, or to the left

Language: To the left

Recto: Forward motion

English: Proceed directly

Además - Close by

English: Adjacent

Placing Food and Drink Orders

Please have a table for two. Una mesa para dos

English: Please, a table for two.

Daily menu: El menú del día

ESL: The daily schedule

Quiero: I'd want to

English: I'd like to

Please take this bill, La Cuenta.

English: Please, the bill

Do they have vegetarian plates? What vegetarian dishes do you offer?

English: What vegetarian dishes do you offer?

If you could have a beer, please.

English: Please have a beer.

Vino tinto/blanco en una copa - A red or white wine glass

Glass of red or white wine, in English

¿Self-gluten options available? - Do you have any options without gluten?

English: Do you have substitutes for gluten?

Existe la propina incluida? - Is the gratuity covered?

Is the gratuity included in English?

Purchasing and mementos

¿Cuánto dice? - What is the price?

English: What is the price?

¿Tiene retraso? Is there a price break?

English: What's the deal?

This is something I would like to purchase.

English: I want to purchase this.

¿Is it possible to work it as a gift? Could you present it as a gift?

Can you package it like a gift, please?

¿Cuál son los antiguos probadores? What location are the changing areas?

Translated: Which way are the changing rooms?

Este tarjeta de crédito se acepta? - Are credit cards accepted here?

English: Are credit cards accepted here?

What size is this? This is what size is it?

In what size is this, in English?

Accidents and Security

Nada ayuda - I require assistance

English: I'm sick.

¡Jailer! - Murderer!

English: Beguir!

¿Cuál es la casa de la policía? - Where is the station of police?

English: Where is the station for the police?

Where's the hospital located? - What location is the hospital?

Eng: What location is the hospital?

A ambulancia, por favor - Would you kindly call for an ambulance?

English: Please call for an ambulance.

Investigating the City

Which places are recommended to visit? Which locations would you suggest seeing?

English: Where would you suggest going?

¿Cuál is el lugar del mirador the closest? What is the closest vantage point?

English: What's the closest vantage point?

¿Cuál es la barrio antigua? What is the route to the ancient town?

How can I go to the old town in English?

What is the best way to get to the beach? - How can I go to the beach the most effectively?

English: Which route gets you to the beach the best?

In what location may I rent a bicycle? - Where do I get a bike to rent?

Where can I rent a bicycle in English?

Existe un parque nío para niños cercano? Is there a kid-friendly park close by?

English: Is there a kid-friendly park close by?

Cultural Sensitivity

¿Sofres de Inglés? - Have you got English?

Do you know how to speak English?

Are you a gallego? - Act

Cultural Sensitivity

Are you a gallego? A Galician speaker, are you?

Can you speak Galician in English?

¿Qué celebraciones locales están llevando a cabo? Which regional celebrations are taking place?

English: What are the upcoming local festivals?

What is the typical Galician dish? - What cuisine is typical in Galicia?

English: What kind of food is typical in Galicia?

What is this place's history? What is this location's history?

English: Could you tell me about this place's past?

¿Cuál es la estación de Santiago? In what manner is the Feast of St. James observed?

English: What is the St. James Feast celebration?

What is the Queimada tradition? - What is the Queimada tradition?

English: What is the Queimada tradition?

Demonstrating gratitude and civility

Ich bin famoso hier - I'm in love here

English: I adore this location.

És muy hermoso/a - It's really lovely

English: It's really lovely.

Muchas gracias por su ayuda - Much appreciation for your assistance

English: I sincerely appreciate your assistance.

I really appreciate that. Thank you so much.

English: Thank you so much.

It's extremely friendly; you are very gracious.

English: How generous of you

How rich/a! . How appetizing!

English: What a tasty treat!

Ya estoy recomendado mucho - I am quite welcome here.

English: I'm really comfortable here.

It's a pleasure to meet you. Es un placer conocerte.

English: I'm glad to have met you.

Unrelated Phrases

¿Será en el baño? How far is the restroom?

Translation: Where's the restroom?

¿Esta mapa me puede ayudar? - I need your assistance with this map.

Can you assist me with this map, please?

What time is it? When is it exactly?

What time is it in English?

I've lost myself, I'm lost.

Translation: I'm lost

No comprendo - I do not comprehend

English: Not sure what you mean.

Could you please repeat that? Would you kindly repeat that?

English: Would you kindly repeat that?

¿Has conectores Wi-Fi? Do you possess Wi-Fi?

English: Wireless internet access?

¿Un billete de transporte público se puede comprar donde? - Where can I get a ticket for public transportation?

English: Where can I get a ticket for public transportation?

¿Puede sugerir un restaurante a mi gusto? - Could you suggest a decent eatery?

English: Could you suggest a decent eatery?

¿Cuál es la marcha de autobís, metro y tren? - How can I go to the rail, bus, or metro stop?

How can I find the bus, metro, or train stop in English?

Adopting the language and culture of Santiago de Compostela can greatly improve your stay and help you build deep relationships with the people. It might be quite helpful to learn and use these frequent phrases in Spanish and Galician to overcome language difficulties and fully immerse oneself in this fascinating city's rich cultural tapestry. These words will open doors to a richer cultural experience and a more enjoyable trip, whether you're going through the quaint streets, dining on delicious Galician food, or just interacting with the friendly locals.

Chapter 4

Safety Essentials in Santiago de Compostela.

It is imperative to obtain comprehensive travel insurance that covers medical emergencies, trip cancellations, and unforeseen incidents before arriving in Santiago de Compostela. A copy of your insurance policy and your emergency contact information should be kept close to hand.

2. Health Safety Measures:

vaccines: You might require certain vaccines or health precautions before visiting Spain, depending on your country of origin and past travel experiences. The World Health Organization (WHO) or your healthcare professional can supply you with the most recent immunization recommendations.

Prescriptions: Make sure you have enough medication for your trip if you take prescription drugs. Always keep prescription drugs in their original, clearly labeled container.

Prepare a compact medical bag with basic supplies like bandages, painkillers, and any personal drugs you might require in case of emergency.

3. Identification and Documentation:

Passport: Always keep your passport safe. Make copies of your passport or scan it digitally, and keep the duplicates apart from the original.

Obtain a valid visa and meet all entry and visa requirements for Spain. Make that the validity of your passport extends past the date of your intended trip.

Identification: When touring the city, bring a copy of your passport or a government-issued photo ID. Make sure your original passport is safely kept in your lodging.

Fourth Party Contacts:

Local Emergency Numbers: Learn the contact details for your nation's embassy or consulate in Spain, as well as local emergency numbers, such as 112, which is Spain's general emergency number.

5. Security of Self:

Safeguard jewels: Keep important papers, cash, and jewels in a hidden pouch or money belt. Keep valuable jewelry and electronics hidden.

Be mindful of your surroundings and remain vigilant, particularly in busy places or popular tourist destinations. Any city can experience pickpocketing, so be mindful of your possessions.

Traveling alone: Give a close friend or relative access to your schedule and contact information if you're going it alone. Periodically check in with them while traveling.

6. Safety of Transportation:

Seat Belts: Whenever you use a vehicle, whether it be a cab or a rented car, you should always buckle up.

Public transportation: Make use of authorized and regulated providers. When getting into a taxi, use caution and make sure the meter is operating or settle on a fare before you go.

Pedestrian Safety: Use approved crossings and pay attention to traffic signals when strolling in Santiago de Compostela. Watch out for drivers and cyclists.

7. Safety of Food and Water:

Food hygiene: Pick dining establishments and restaurants that follow hygienic procedures. Eat only fully cooked food; do not eat seafood that is raw or undercooked.

Bottled Water: For peace of mind, some travelers choose bottled water even though the tap water in Santiago de Compostela is usually safe to drink. When buying bottled water, be sure the seal is intact.

Moderate and responsible alcohol consumption is advised. Always watch your drink, and exercise caution while receiving beverages from strangers.

8. Help for Emergencies:

Medical Facilities: Learn where the hospitals and other medical facilities are located in Santiago de Compostela. To get help in the event of a medical emergency, dial 112.

Language Barrier: Although English is widely spoken in Santiago de Compostela, it's still beneficial to know a few basic Spanish words so that you can communicate in an emergency.

In Santiago de Compostela, How to Remain Safe

1. Cultural Awareness:

Honor Local Traditions: Santiago de Compostela is a culturally and historically rich city. When visiting churches and other places of worship, especially, be mindful of the local customs and religious practices.

When venturing into locations that are religious or conservative, it is advisable to dress modestly. Please show respect for the local way of life by covering your knees and shoulders.

2. Climatic Awareness

Variable Weather: The weather in Galicia is not always predictable. Especially if you're traveling during the rainier seasons, be ready for rain. Keep a raincoat or umbrella with you.

Precautions for Hiking: If you intend to hike the Camino de Santiago, be mindful of the local weather and adopt the appropriate safety measures. Wear layers of clothing and bring necessary items such as a first aid kit, map, and compass.

3. Hazards from nature:

Tides & Beach Safety: Be mindful of the tides and observe safety precautions when swimming if you plan to visit the coastal regions close to Santiago de Compostela. On beaches, heed the warning flags.

Hiking Safety: If you go through undeveloped areas, stick to designated pathways and observe safety precautions. Tell someone what you're going trekking, and don't forget to pack snacks and water.

Chapter 5

Mastering Money and Budgeting for Your Santiago de Compostela Vacation

In the center of Galicia, Spain, a visit to Santiago de Compostela offers a fascinating fusion of history, culture, and spiritual discovery. Making the most of your financial resources or being frugal when traveling are two reasons why planning and handling money well are essential for a stress-free and pleasurable trip. We will explore efficient methods of cutting costs, setting up a specific budget, and optimizing your financial preparation for your trip to Santiago de Compostela in this extensive book.

Choosing Your Financial Objectives

1. Choose Your Mode of Transportation:

Budget Travel: Choose this as your main mode of transportation if you're on a tight budget and want to stay put and eat at reasonably priced restaurants and activities.

Mid-Range trip: This is the type of trip you should choose if you can afford to pay moderately and want to strike a balance between comfort and value.

Luxury Travel: Identify this as your favorite type of travel if you're prepared to splurge on first-rate experiences and don't care as much about your budget.

2. Determine Experiences That Are Must-See and Must-Do:

Make a list of the must-see sights, things to do, and experiences you will have in Santiago de Compostela. Give these experiences top priority while creating your budget.

3. Assign a Reasonable Budget:

For your entire vacation, decide on a reasonable budget based on your preferred way of travel and the things you simply must see. Think about spending areas including lodging, meals, travel, entertainment, and other ancillary costs.

4. Establish a Safety Deposit Box:

Set aside some money from your budget for unforeseen costs, crises, or opportunities that might come up while you're traveling.

Cost-Cutting Techniques

1. Making travel and lodging arrangements:

Plan Ahead: Getting your travel and lodging together as soon as possible will usually result in a discount. Keep an eye out for deals on hotels and airlines.

Adaptable Travel Dates: Be adaptable while choosing your trip dates. More economical solutions may be found by traveling on weekdays or during the shoulder season.

Use Fare Comparison Websites: To locate the best offers on travel and lodging, make use of fare comparison websites and apps. To get loyalty credits, think about making direct hotel and airline reservations.

Examine Alternatives: Look for less expensive flights and accommodations at neighboring cities and alternate airports.

2. conveyance:

Public Transit: To move around the city, take one of the many public transportation choices, such as buses or trams. It is easy to get around Santiago de Compostela by public transportation.

Bike and Walk: A lot of Santiago de Compostela's attractions are close to one another by foot. Another affordable and environmentally beneficial option to get around the city is to rent a bike.

Steer Clear of high Hours: To save money on transportation, steer clear of high traffic hours while hiring a car or hailing a cab.

3. Modifications:

Hostels and Guesthouses: As they are frequently less expensive than hotels, consider booking accommodations at hostels or guesthouses. There are several reasonably priced lodging alternatives available in Santiago de Compostela.

Booking Sites: Check prices and read other travelers' reviews on online booking sites. Check these platforms for any deals or promotions.

Apartment Rentals: If you're traveling in a group or for extended periods of time, renting an independent apartment can be a cost-effective option.

Examine Loyalty Programs: To obtain benefits and savings, think about enrolling in hotel companies' loyalty programs if you often stay at their establishments.

4. Eating

Local Eateries: For a more affordable dining experience than at tourist-oriented enterprises, visit local cafes and restaurants for real food.

"Menu del Dia": During lunch, several establishments provide daily menu options. Look for them. These reasonably priced fixed-price menus frequently have several dishes.

Self-Catering: If your lodging permits it, make some of your meals and get groceries from neighborhood stores. This can reduce the cost of eating out.

5. Events and Points of Interest:

Free Attractions: Make use of the free attractions, like strolling around Santiago de Compostela's old streets or going to the city's parks and squares.

Ascertain whether Santiago de Compostela provides cheap entry to a number of sites and public transit by checking for city cards.

Tours Guided: To select the most affordable options for guided tours, check costs and read reviews.

6. Banking and Currency Exchange:

ATM Withdrawals: When necessary, take out local money (euros) from Santiago de Compostela's ATMs. This frequently offers a good exchange rate.

Exchange offices for currencies: Check rates there, but beware of exorbitant fees and commissions.

Credit Cards: To benefit from advantageous exchange rates, use credit cards for larger purchases. However, be mindful of any potential foreign transaction costs levied by your bank.

Download currency conversion applications to stay up to date on real-time exchange rates and spending.

7. Regional Rebates and Promotions:

Look into whether Santiago de Compostela has tourist cards that offer savings on lodging, dining, and transportation.

Student and Senior savings: Check with museums, attractions, and transportation providers about any possible savings you may be eligible for if you're a student or a senior.

8. Interaction:

Wi-Fi: Rather than utilizing cell data for communication, make use of the free Wi-Fi that is accessible at many cafes, restaurants, and lodging establishments.

Local SIM Card: Buying a local SIM card for your phone can be a more economical option if you need mobile data than roaming with your home operator.

9. Insurance for Travel:

When it comes to making sure your journey to Santiago de Compostela is both safe and pleasurable, travel insurance is an essential part of your financial planning. When getting travel insurance, keep the following things in mind:

Types of Coverage:

Medical Coverage: Verify that full medical coverage is included in your travel insurance policy. This ought to include hospital stays, doctor visits, medical emergencies, and any required medical evacuations.

vacation Cancellation/Interruption: Should you need to cancel or shorten your vacation because of unanticipated circumstances, illness, or injury, your travel insurance should cover you.

Lost or Delayed Baggage: Personal belongings and lost or delayed luggage should be replaced at the expense of the insurance.

Trip Delays: Seek coverage that reimburses you for costs, such lodging and meals, that you incur as a result of travel delays.

Liability coverage: This safeguards you in the event that, while traveling, you unintentionally destroy property or hurt someone else.

Make sure your insurance provides emergency help around-the-clock, including a hotline for medical situations and assistance with travel.

Coverage Edges

Understand the coverage limitations for the various insurance components. Know how much your coverage will cover, for instance, in the event of medical expenditures or trip cancellation.

Pre-existing Health Issues:

Tell your insurance company about any pre-existing medical illnesses you may have, and make sure you have the required waivers in place or that your ailments are covered.

Destinations of Travel:

Verify that your travel insurance includes coverage for Santiago de Compostela and your particular location. particular regions may be restricted by particular policies.

Time Spent Covering:

Find out the precise dates of your trip and make sure your insurance will cover you for the full duration of the trip, including any extensions you may like to take.

The price of insurance

To locate an insurance plan that provides the required coverage at a fair price, compare quotes from several insurance companies. Remember that the least expensive choice could not offer sufficient coverage.

Limitations & Exclusions:

To comprehend the limitations and exclusions, carefully read the policy. Coverage for extreme sports or specific high-risk activities are examples of common exclusions.

Documents and Points of Contact:

Throughout your vacation, carry copies of your insurance card (either digital or physical), your policy, and your emergency contact details with you at all times.

Procedures for Claims:

Become familiar with the process involved in submitting a claim. Understand the necessary paperwork and how to get in touch with your insurance company in an emergency.

Who to Contact in an Emergency:

Keep your insurance company's emergency number on file on your phone and give it to a family member or close friend.

Keep in mind that travel insurance is an important safety precaution that can offer monetary security in unforeseen circumstances. Even though it raises the cost of your vacation, it provides piece of mind and guarantees that unanticipated events won't ruin your trip to Santiago de Compostela.

Cash and The Budget.

Managing your finances and creating a budget for your Santiago de Compostela holiday involves more than just saving money—it also involves maximizing your expenditures to get the most out of your trip. You may have a stress-free and unforgettable trip to this enchanted city by putting money-saving measures in place, sticking to a well-planned budget, and making clear financial goals. Keep yourself updated about local deals, currency exchange rates, and strategies to stretch your travel spending. You can tour Santiago de Compostela and manage your funds at the same time if you plan ahead and practice sound financial management. Travel safely!

Chapter 6

Navigating Santiago de Compostela: A Comprehensive Guide to Transportation Options, Budgeting, Car Rental, and Owning Your Own Car on Tour.

The northern Spanish province of Galicia's capital, Santiago de Compostela, is a spiritual, cultural, and historical mecca. Knowing your mobility options is crucial for a successful visit, whether you're a tourist enjoying this stunning region or a pilgrim traveling the Camino de Santiago. We'll cover everything from how to get around Santiago de Compostela to budgeting tips, the advantages and disadvantages of renting a car, and driving your own car to explore the city and its surroundings in this extensive guide.

Section 1: Santiago de Compostela Transportation Options

1.1 Strolling:

The best way to explore Santiago de Compostela's historic core is on foot. The city is pedestrian-friendly. Numerous sites, such as the well-known Santiago Cathedral, are easily accessible by foot.

1.2 Transit in Public:

Santiago features a well-functioning public transit network that includes both buses and cabs. Buses have clearly established routes and schedules, making them an inexpensive means of transportation to various regions of the city.

1.3 Limos:

In Santiago, taxis are widely available and can be reserved in advance or hailed on the street. They can be more costly than other options, but they are practical for swiftly moving about the city.

1.4% Cycling:

With an expanding network of bike lanes across the city, cycling is a practical way to get around

Santiago. There are several rental shops where you may pick up a bike, or you can use the city's bike-sharing program.

1.5 Rent a Car:

The Galician countryside and Santiago may be easily explored with greater freedom and ease when you rent a car. The next part will cover car rentals in more detail.

Section 2: Transportation Budgeting

2.1 Costs of Public Transportation:

One-way costs on Santiago's public buses are usually less than €2, making them moderately cheap. Since taxi fares can be higher, it's important to plan your budget appropriately.

2.2 Strolling:

Walking about the city is the most economical way to see it because there are no transportation expenses.

In 2.3 Bike:

The cost of renting a bike can range from €10 to €25 per day, depending on the kind and length of the rental.

2.4 Cost of a Rental Car:

Rates for renting a car in Santiago de Compostela vary according to the kind of vehicle, length of stay, and rental company. A compact automobile will typically cost you between €30 and €50 per day.

2.5 Price of Fuel:

Consider gasoline prices whether you intend to use your own vehicle or rent one. Although it might vary, gas prices in Spain are often higher than in many other European nations.

Section 3: Santiago de Compostela Car Rental

3.1 Benefits of Hiring a Car:

Flexibility: Having a car rental allows you to drive at your own speed while exploring Santiago and the Galician region. You can travel to far-flung towns, beaches, and natural areas that would be harder to get to by public transportation.

Convenience: Renting a car is a convenient alternative, particularly for families or bigger parties, as it makes it easy to carry luggage and shopping items.

Time Efficiency: By eschewing the public transit schedules and stops, you can make the most of your time.

3.2 Selecting a Rental Company:

Numerous international and local automobile rental companies are available in Santiago de Compostela. To select a trustworthy firm that meets your needs, compare rates, terms of rental, and customer testimonials.

3.3 On the road in Santiago:

Become familiar with the laws governing traffic in your area before you get behind the wheel). When driving through Santiago's historic center, exercise caution as there are tight streets and restricted places.

3.4 Car Park:

There are several parking choices available in Santiago, such as garages, public parking lots, and street parking. A few hotels further offer parking. Recall that there can be parking costs.

3.5 Coverage:

To guard against unanticipated events, comprehensive insurance is recommended while renting a vehicle.

Part 4: Driving Your Own Vehicle While on Tour

4.1 Perks of Bringing Your Own Vehicle:

Comfort: If you're used to operating a vehicle on your own, you could find navigating Santiago and its environs easier.

Cost-Effectiveness: Bringing your own vehicle instead of renting one will save costs if you're going on a lengthy tour of Europe.

Convenience: Possessing a car allows you to transport your possessions, such as camping equipment or other necessities for trip.

4.2 Pointers for Driving Your Own Vehicle:

Vehicle Suitability: Make sure your car is appropriate for the type of terrain you intend to drive. There may be unpaved roads in some rural places.

Verify sure the documentation for your car is current and conforms with Spanish regulations, including the insurance and registration.

Parking and Security: Look for safe places to park in Santiago and other places. Take into account lodging options that include private parking.

4.3 Spain's Driving Rules:

Spain has unique traffic laws and signage. Learn about these rules and make sure you have the required paperwork, like your driver's license and car registration.

4.4 Navigation and Language:

Even though there are a lot of Spanish and Galician road signs, using a GPS or guidance program can be very beneficial. Ensure that your app or navigation gadget is functional in Spain.
In summary:

A range of transportation choices are available in Santiago de Compostela to accommodate various tastes and price ranges. Careful planning is necessary whether you decide to walk, take public transportation, hire a car, or bring your own. Think over the benefits and drawbacks of each option, set aside money appropriately, and make sure you're ready for an amazing trip

around this lovely city and the Galician region.
Travel safely!

Chapter 7

Arriving in Santiago de Compostela: The Ultimate Guide to Flight Options, Airport Arrival, Accommodation Choices, and Exploring Friendly Neighborhoods.

The spiritual center of Galicia, Spain, Santiago de Compostela, entices both pilgrims and visitors with its illustrious past, breathtaking architecture, and lively culture. If you prepare ahead of time, arriving in Santiago may be a smooth and interesting experience. In this extensive guide, we will go over the best and safest travel alternatives, offer advice on how to get around Santiago de Compostela Airport, talk about lodging possibilities, including staying close to the airport, and introduce you to welcoming districts in Galicia.

Section 1: Santiago de Compostela Flight Options

1.1 Direct Travel:

Direct flights are available from major European cities like Madrid, Barcelona, Paris, London, and Frankfurt to Santiago de Compostela Airport (SCQ). The easiest and fastest option are frequently direct flights.

1.2 Converging Aircraft:

You might have to take a connecting flight via a major European hub, such as Madrid, Barcelona, or Lisbon, if you're going from outside of Europe. While there may be less flexibility in terms of airline options, this may result in longer journey times.

Section 1.3: Selecting the Safest and Best Airlines

Numerous European airlines, including Lufthansa, Ryanair, Iberia, and Vueling, offer service to Santiago de Compostela. Usually, these airlines uphold strict safety regulations.

1.4 Safety Procedures at Airports:

Santiago de Compostela Airport guarantees a safe and pleasant arrival experience by adhering to international safety standards and regulations. Arriving at Santiago de Compostela Airport in Section 2

2.1 Facilities at Airports:

Santiago Airport has a lot of amenities, including stores, restaurants, currency exchange counters, baggage claim, and car rental services. It is a contemporary airport.

2.2 Traveling to the City Center from the Airport:

The airport is roughly 10 kilometers (6 miles) from Santiago's city center. There are various ways you can get to the city center:

Taxi: Outside the airport, taxis are easily accessible. The trip takes 20 minutes and costs between €20 and €30 to get to the city core.

Shuttle Bus from the Airport: There is a regular shuttle bus service from the airport to the city center. It's a practical and reasonably priced choice.

Rental Car: You can pick up a car at the airport if you want to drive about a lot and see the area. In the terminal are rental desks.

2.3 How to Get About the Airport:

Santiago Airport is easy to traverse because of its tiny size. There is both English and Spanish language signage. Most of the staff members are helpful and kind.

Section 3: Santiago de Compostela Lodging Options

3.1 Hotels in City Center:

If you choose to stay in the city center, you may fully experience Santiago's allure. Parador de Santiago, Hotel San Francisco Monumento, and

Hotel Compostela are a few well regarded choices.

3.2 Hotels at Airports:

If you have early or late flights, or just want a more laid-back vibe, you might want to book a hotel close to the airport. The Santiago Airport Hotel is a handy option because it's close to the terminal.

3.3 Guesthouses and Homestays:

Santiago provides a range of guesthouses and homestays that offer a genuine experience. Numerous possibilities are listed for every budget on websites like Booking.com and Airbnb.

3.4 Inexpensive Lodging Options:

Budget-conscious tourists can find less expensive lodging options like Hotel Bonaval or hostels like The Last Stamp Hostel.

Section 4: Santiago de Compostela's Amiable Neighborhoods

4.1 Old Town/Casco Antiguo:

Santiago's Old Town, which is home to the city's iconic Santiago Cathedral, attractive streets, and historic squares, is its center. This district is a must-see, with an abundance of stores and eateries.
San Pedro (4.2):

The bustling area of San Pedro is well-known for its open-air markets, where you can sample authentic Galician food. For foodies, the San Pedro Market is a culinary haven.
4.3 Bonaval, Santo Domingo:

The Cidade da Cultura center for modern art and Bonaval Park are located in this area. It provides a blend of calm and sophistication.
4.4 Lazaro Santo:

San Lázaro, which is close to the airport, provides quick access to both the airport and the city center as well as a tranquil setting. It's a fantastic choice for guests looking for a more sedate stay.

Tips for a Stress-Free Arrival in Santiago de Compostela, Section 5

5.1 Documentation and Visa:

Make sure you have the travel permits and visas required to enter Spain.

5.2 Exchange of Currency:

To pay for immediate costs like transportation and meals, exchange some money at the airport.

5.3 Terminology:

Galician is also widely spoken there, even though Spanish is the official language. It can be useful to know a few simple Spanish phrases for communication.

5.4 City Transportation:

To have unrestricted access to the local buses and trams throughout your visit, think about getting a Santiago Card.

5.5 Insurance for Travel:

Always carry trip cancellation and emergency medical coverage when traveling.

The beginning of an amazing journey in this historically significant and culturally rich city is arriving in Santiago de Compostela. You may maximize your trip to Santiago and discover the friendliness and warmth of Galicia by picking the finest travel options, navigating the airport with ease, booking appropriate lodging, and touring pleasant areas. Travel safely!

Chapter 8

The Rules

Navigating Santiago de Compostela: Laws and Ethics for Visitors.

World travelers are welcomed to Santiago de Compostela, a spiritual and historically rich city. It is imperative that travelers keep themselves informed about local laws and ethical principles in order to guarantee a peaceful and courteous experience for all. We will go over the rules, regulations, and moral guidelines that tourists should be aware of and follow when visiting Santiago de Compostela in this book, which will help you behave politely and respectfully throughout the city.

Section 1: Overarching Principles

1.1 Deference to Houses of Religion:

The city of Santiago de Compostela holds great religious importance. When visiting places of worship such as the Santiago Cathedral, dress modestly and behave with decency. In the cathedral, quiet is usually expected.

1.2 Public Conduct and Noise:

Particularly in residential areas and during the siesta hours, which are normally from 2:00 PM to 5:00 PM, keep noise levels down. Honor the peace that the city and its people have to offer.

1.3 Waste Management and Litter:

Litter should be disposed of in these bins. Keep the parks and streets tidy. There are recycling centers located all around the city.

1.4 Intoxication in Public:

Disruptive behavior and public intoxication are not accepted. Drink alcohol in moderation, especially while you're in public.

Part 2: Security and Safety

2.1 Services for Emergency:

In Spain, 112 is the universal emergency number to call in case of emergency. To contact the police, ambulance, and fire departments, dial this number.

2.2 Security of Self:

Though typically safe, Santiago de Compostela is still a city, so proceed with caution as you would in any urban area. Pay close attention to your possessions, particularly in crowded places.

2.3 Rules Regarding Traffic:

Pedestrian security is crucial. When crossing roadways, use the marked crosswalks and pay attention to traffic signals. On the city's paths, keep an eye out for motorized scooters and bikers.

2.4 Medical Institutions:

In case you have medical emergencies, become familiar with the locations of healthcare services, including pharmacies and hospitals.

Section 3: Moral Principles

3.1 Protocol for the Camino de Santiago:

Follow the "leave no trace" philosophy if you are walking the Camino de Santiago. Honor the local communities, your fellow pilgrims, and the environment. Acquire a pilgrim's credential in order to gather stamps, or sellos, along the route.

3.2 Privacy and Photography:

Honor people's privacy when snapping pictures in public areas. Prior to taking any kind of picture of someone, especially in a private context, always get their consent.

3.3 Terminology:

Even though many tourist destinations speak English, locals value knowing some basic Spanish phrases or Galician, the indigenous tongue. Since courtesy is universal, say "Hola" (hello) or "Buenos días" (good morning) to everyone you meet.

3.4 Gratuity:

In Spain, tipping is not as customary as it is in several other nations. In cafés and restaurants, it's typical to round up the amount or leave little change. Superior service could be worth a larger gratuity.

Section 4: Law and Organization

4.1 Legal Drugs:

It is against the law to possess or use recreational drugs in Spain. For offenses involving drugs, there are strict consequences.

4.2 Automobile Laws:

Learn about Spanish traffic laws if you intend to rent a car or take other forms of transportation. Keep an eye on the speed limits, buckle up, and don't text and drive.

Tobacco Laws:

In Spain, the legal drinking age is eighteen. It is not advised to drink in public and can result in fines, particularly in parks and squares.

4.4 Preservation of Cultural Property:

Defacing or removing cultural and historical property is forbidden. This comprises artifacts discovered along the Camino de Santiago path, which have to be preserved.

Section 5: Dining Habits and Customs

5.1 Make Diner Reservations:

Making reservations at restaurants is an excellent idea, particularly during busy eating times. This guarantees you a table, especially in busy restaurants.

5.2 Hours of Meal:

Spanish people have a distinct eating regimen. Dinner is normally served from 8:30 PM to 10:30 PM or later, while lunch is usually served from 1:30 PM to 3:30 PM. Make food plans that work for you.

5.3 Divided Bills and Tapas:

Ordering a drink at a bar or restaurant typically includes a complimentary tapa, which is a tiny snack. It's not always the case that splitting the bill is automatic when dining in a group, so make sure to inquire.

Section 6: Buying and Keeping Memorabilia

6.1 Retail Hours:

The majority of stores in Santiago de Compostela close for a few hours in the afternoon in observance of the siesta timetable. Make appropriate plans for your shopping and confirm the store's hours of operation.

6.2 Tax-Exempt Purchasing:

Value Added Tax (VAT) refunds are frequently available to non-residents of the European Union on qualifying transactions. Seek out stores with the Tax-Free Shopping sign up and request the required paperwork.

Section 7: Regional Traditions and Customs

7.1 Customs of Galicia:

Learn about the traditions and customs of the area. Galicia has a vibrant cultural history that includes dance, music, and festivals. When appropriate, honor these customs and take part in them.

7.2 Respect for Pilgrimage:

Be mindful of people who are strolling the Camino de Santiago even if you are not a pilgrim. Avoid getting in the way of their travels and offer support or encouragement when required.

As you set out on your tour through Santiago de Compostela, keep in mind that following ethical standards and honoring local regulations are crucial to a satisfying and enjoyable experience. In addition to ensuring your safety, you can help ensure that residents and visitors live in harmony in this stunning and culturally diverse city by adhering to certain guidelines and rules. Your journey to Santiago de Compostela will be enjoyable and fulfilling if you approach it with knowledge and respect.

Chapter 9

Accommodation Options in Santiago de Compostela: A Comprehensive Guide with Budgeting Tips for Rentals, Homestays, and Hotels

As the last point on the Camino de Santiago pilgrimage, Santiago de Compostela, the capital of Galicia in northern Spain, draws visitors from all over the world who come to study its rich history, vibrant culture, and spiritual significance. Selecting the ideal lodging will improve your time in this enchanting city. We will examine the many lodging choices in Santiago de Compostela, such as hotels, homestays, and rentals, in this extensive guide, along with some budgeting advice to help you get the most out of your trip.

Section 1: Santiago de Compostela Lodging Options

1.1 Lodgings:

There are many different types of hotels in Santiago, ranging from opulent properties to more affordable choices. Hotels are a convenient option for tourists since they offer a variety of amenities, such as bars, restaurants, and concierge services.

1.2 Guesthouses and Homestays:

In Santiago, staying with locals can offer a fully comprehensive cultural experience. Guesthouses and homestays frequently provide a more intimate experience and the chance to interact with locals.

1.3 Holiday Homes:

A house, an apartment, or a cottage can all be rented for a vacation, providing a home away from home. They're especially well-liked by those who want to stay longer or who want a quiet, autonomous place to stay.

1.4 Lodgings:

For individuals on a tight budget, lone travelers, backpackers, or those who want to meet other travelers, hostels are an affordable option. There are numerous clean hostels in Santiago that offer both private rooms and dorms.

Section 2: Accommodation Budgeting

2.1 Lodging Fees:

The location, star rating, and season all have a big impact on hotel costs in Santiago. While upmarket accommodations may cost more than €150 per night, inexpensive hotels typically range in price from €50 to €100.

2.2 The Price of Guesthouses and Homestays:

The cost of a night in a homestay or guesthouse might vary from €30 to €80, based on the facilities and degree of comfort provided.

2.3 Costs of Vacation Rentals:

The cost of a vacation rental might vary, with choices ranging from €40 to €150 or more per night. Longer stays could qualify for savings.

Costs of Hostels: 2.4

With dormitory beds starting at around €15 to €30, hostels are the most affordable choice. Hostels also provide private rooms, but at a slightly higher price.

2.5 Extra Charges:

Consciously consider extra costs like city taxes, cleaning fees (for holiday rentals), and breakfast fees (at some hotels). Include these in your spending plan.

Section 3: Santiago de Compostela Hotel Accommodations

3.1 Exotic lodgings:

Santiago is home to a number of opulent hotels with first-rate features including spas, great eating establishments, and breathtaking vistas. The Parador de Santiago and Hotel Palacio del Carmen are two notable choices.

3.2 In-between Hotels:

Budget and comfort are nicely balanced in mid-range hotels. In this category, Hotel San Francisco Monumento and Hotel Compostela are popular options.

3.3 Inexpensive Hotel Options:

Comfortable lodging is available for guests on a budget at establishments like Hotel Bonaval and Hotel Rey Fernando.

Section 4: Guesthouses and Homestays

4.1 Advantages of Guesthouses and Homestays:

Experience Local: Living with people from the area gives you a genuine window into Galician culture and daily life.

Personalized Service: To make your stay more enjoyable, hosts frequently provide tailored advice and suggestions.

Cost-effectiveness: Compared to hotels, homestays and guesthouses may be more affordable.

4.2 Reserving Guesthouses and Homestays:

There are many different homestays and guesthouses in Santiago de Compostela listed on websites like Airbnb, Booking.com, and HomeAway.

Check reviews and get in touch with hosts to make sure you have a relaxing stay.

Section 5: Hired Vacation Homes

5.1 Categories of Cottages for Rent:

In Santiago, you can rent out houses, flats, cottages, and even old townhouses for your vacation.

Select a rental that fits the size of your group and the amount of privacy you want.

5.2 Vacation Rental Reservations:

Websites like as Booking.com, Airbnb, and Vrbo provide a huge assortment of vacation rentals in Santiago.

Take note of the cancellation rules, reviews, and property descriptions.

Section Six: Housing

6.1 Hostel Advantages:

Affordability: For tourists on a tight budget, hostels are an affordable option.

Social Atmosphere: Meeting other tourists is made easier by the social events and activities that hostels frequently arrange.

6.2 Well-Known Santiago Hostels:

Both Blanco Albergue and The Last Stamp Hostel are well-known hostels with private room and dorm options.

Section 7: Extra Advice on Planning and Scheduling

7.1 Reserve in Advance:

Especially during the busiest travel seasons, making reservations in advance can help you get a better deal on availability and lodging.

7.2 Adjustable Times:

If your vacation dates are changeable, think about changing your itinerary to coincide with a period when lodging costs are less.

7.3 Bundle Offers:

Package packages that bundle lodging, airfare, and activities are available on certain travel websites, and they may help you save money.

A wide variety of lodging choices are available in Santiago de Compostela to accommodate different spending limits and tastes. Careful preparation and budgeting are essential to guaranteeing a pleasant and pleasurable stay in this historic and culturally diverse city, regardless of whether you choose to stay in a hotel, homestay, vacation rental, or hostel. Through careful consideration of the elements described in this guide, you will be able to thoroughly immerse yourself in Santiago de Compostela's unique experience. Travel safely!

Chapter 10

The Best Time to Visit Santiago de Compostela: Ideal Weather and Memorable Experiences.

Santiago de Compostela is a city with a rich history, breathtaking architecture, and profound spiritual significance. It is situated in the Galicia area of northwest Spain. When you visit this fascinating city will have a big influence on how you feel about it. To assist you in organizing the ideal vacation for an unforgettable experience, we will examine the ideal time to visit Santiago de Compostela in this extensive guide, taking into consideration local weather, cultural events, and the Camino de Santiago pilgrimage.

Section 1: Comprehending the Climate of Santiago

1.1 Synopsis of Climate:

Santiago de Compostela's closeness to the Atlantic Ocean contributes to its maritime mild climate. All year long, the climate is defined by high humidity, pleasant temperatures, and moderate rainfall.

1.2 Ranges of Temperature:

The average daily temperature in the city during the mild winters ranges from 8°C to 15°C (46°F to 59°F). Warm summers are experienced, with typical daily highs of 18°C to 25°C (64°F to 77°F).

1.3 Irrigation:

Rainfall in Santiago is modest, with November and December being the wettest months. The summers in the city are rather dry, which makes them perfect for outdoor exploration.

Section 2: The Optimal Weather Conditions

Springtime (April–June):

With its lovely weather, spring is probably the best time to visit Santiago de Compostela. The city comes alive at this time of year with verdant surroundings, blossoming flowers, and comfortable weather. The typical daytime temperature is between 15°C and 20°C, or 59°F and 68°F. Another popular season for pilgrims traveling the Camino de Santiago is the spring.

Remarkable Occasions:

Take in Santiago's rich religious traditions during the processions of Holy Week (Semana Santa), which take place in late March or early April.
Take advantage of summertime crowds and engage in outdoor activities such as hiking and exploring the city's lovely streets.
Participate in cultural festivals and activities such as the May International Documentary Film Festival (Curtocircuíto).
2.2 July–August, or Summer:

The summer months in Santiago de Compostela are the busiest travel times because of the pleasant weather and longer daylight hours. The typical daily temperature is between 18°C and 25°C, or 64°F and 77°F.

Remarkable Occasions:

Every day at noon, the Pilgrim's Mass is celebrated in the Santiago Cathedral, where you can see the gigantic incense burner, known as the Botafumeiro, swing.
Enjoy bands, fireworks, and a joyous atmosphere on July 25th at the Santiago Apostol Festival (Festas do Apóstolo).
In the summertime sun, stroll among the parks, gardens, and outdoor cafes of the city.
Section 3: Seasons Off-Peak for Exceptional Encounters

3.1 Fall: September to November

Santiago de Compostela is best visited in the fall, especially if you want to avoid the crowds and enjoy colder temperatures. The typical daytime temperature is between 15°C and 22°C, or 59°F and 72°F.

Remarkable Occasions:

Watch the parks and gardens throughout the city change as the leaves begin to turn tones of gold and red.
Discover the Old Town's historic avenues and landmarks in a more sedate setting.
Visit the San Froilán Festival in October, which offers traditional Galician cuisine, music, and cultural events.
3.2 Winter: From December to February

Because of the occasional downpour and lower temperatures, winter is the least popular season for tourists visiting Santiago de Compostela. The typical daytime temperature is between 8°C and 15°C (46°F and 59°F).

Remarkable Occasions:

Savor a substantial Galician stew or hot chocolate in one of the city's charming cafes while you take in the warm ambiance.

Discover the Camino de Santiago in the slower paced winter months and take in a more contemplative walk.

Section 4: Particular Recommendations for the Camino de Santiago Trek

4.1 Pilgrimage in the Spring and Autumn:

The better weather and agreeable temperatures during the spring and autumn months make the Camino de Santiago a popular choice for pilgrims. There are fewer weather extremes throughout these seasons, making hiking comfortable.

Remarkable Occasions:

Make connections with pilgrims from all over the world and enjoy the friendly atmosphere of the Camino walk.

See Galicia's breathtaking scenery as you travel in the direction of Santiago de Compostela.

Considerations for the Summer:

The Camino de Santiago is most popular in the summer, although it may also be very hot and congested during that time. Along the route, be ready for increasing heat and the likelihood of restricted lodgings.

Remarkable Occasions:

Savor the joyous ambiance of the Camino in the summer, when a greater number of pilgrims exchange tales and firsthand accounts.
Savor more daylight hours for leisurely strolls and exploring.
Final Thoughts for a Remarkable Visit in Section 5

5.1 Reservations for Lodging:

It's a good idea to reserve your lodging in advance, regardless of the season you pick, particularly for Camino pilgrims and during popular travel times.
5.2 Clothes in Layers:

Because Santiago's weather is unpredictable, bring layers.

Layered Apparel:

Because Santiago's weather can change quickly, bring layers that you can wear to accommodate shifting conditions. Wearing clothing that is lightweight and breathable is crucial to ensure comfort whether touring the city or walking the Camino. For outdoor activities, think about bringing along a waterproof jacket and cozy walking or hiking boots.

5.3 Rain Gear and Umbrellas:

Rain can fall in Santiago during the best seasons as well. Bring a small umbrella or a raincoat in case of sudden downpours to keep dry.

Sun Protection (5.4):

During the summer, wear a wide-brimmed hat, sunglasses, and sunscreen to protect yourself from the sun. Sunglasses and a hat are still helpful on sunny days in other seasons.

5.5 Honor regional customs:

It is considerate to dress modestly if you intend to visit churches or attend religious events. Wear anything that covers your knees and shoulders.
5.6 Speaking Abilities:

Although many Santiago de Compostela residents understand English, getting to know a few basic Spanish phrases will improve your stay and make interacting with locals more pleasurable.

Whether you are looking for excellent weather or a chance to engage in distinctive cultural activities, the best time to visit Santiago de Compostela ultimately depends on your choices. A perfect combination of nice weather, cultural events, and the chance to see the Camino de Santiago pilgrimage may be found in the spring and fall. Even though it is the busiest season, summer offers more daylight hours and a vibrant atmosphere. Autumn and winter, on the other hand, provide a calmer, more reflective atmosphere.

No matter the season, Santiago de Compostela beckons travelers with its breathtaking architecture, rich history, and friendly Galician culture. You may plan a memorable vacation that fits your interests and preferences by thinking about your top travel priorities and using the advice in this guide. Whether you decide to walk the Camino de Santiago pilgrimage, tour the city's medieval streets, or attend cultural events, Santiago de Compostela guarantees an unforgettable and enlightening experience.

The Best Time to Visit Santiago de Compostela with Family and Loved Ones for a Memorable Experience.

With its rich history, culture, and spirituality, Santiago de Compostela is the ideal place to spend quality time with loved ones and make treasured family memories. When you visit this magical city will have a big influence on how good your experience is. The perfect time to visit Santiago de Compostela with your family and friends will be discussed in this extensive guide, which takes into account the ideal weather, family-friendly activities, cultural events, and the Camino de Santiago pilgrimage.

Understanding Santiago's Family-Friendly Attractions (Section 1)

1.1 The Cathedral of Santiago:

The Santiago Cathedral, sometimes referred to as the Cathedral of Saint James, is a must-see sight that combines architectural beauty with spiritual significance. Families can marvel at the giant incense burner, Botafumeiro, and tour the beautiful interior, which includes the Portico de la Gloria.

In 1.2 The Park at Alameda:

Alameda Park is a charming green area in the heart of the city that's ideal for relaxed family outings, picnics, and strolls. It offers a peaceful diversion from Santiago's busy streets.

1.3 Aquapark Casa del Agua:

Casa del Agua is an aqua park featuring pools, water slides, and leisure spaces that is great for family outings. It's a fantastic summertime method of staying cool.

1.4 La Museo das Peregrinaciones e de Santiago, or the Science Museum:

This interactive museum has interesting displays that both adults and kids will enjoy. It offers information about the customs of the city and the history of the Camino de Santiago pilgrimage.

1.5 Playgrounds and Parks:

There are lots of parks and playgrounds in Santiago where kids may run about and have fun. Families often choose Parque da Alameda and Parque Eugenio Granell.

Section 2: The Optimal Weather Conditions

Springtime (April–June):

A family trip to Santiago de Compostela is best done in the spring. The city is decked up in blossoming flowers, verdant foliage, and pleasant weather during this time of year. The typical daytime temperature is between 15°C and 20°C, or 59°F and 68°F.

Remarkable Occasions:

When the weather is nice, families of all ages can enjoy exploring the Santiago Cathedral and its surroundings.
have strolls around Alameda Park, where families may have picnics and children can play.

Experience the lively atmosphere of local festivals and cultural events, which are often held in the spring and allow families to fully immerse themselves in Galician customs.

2.2 July–August, or Summer:

The summer months in Santiago de Compostela are the busiest travel times because of the pleasant weather and longer daylight hours. The typical daily temperature is between 18°C and 25°C, or 64°F and 77°F.

Remarkable Occasions:

Go to the Santiago Cathedral for the daily Pilgrim's Mass and take in the breathtaking view of the Botafumeiro swing overhead.

Enjoy the vibrant summertime vibe of the city, which includes festivals, outdoor cafes, and street performers.

Dine at family-friendly eateries serving delectable Galician cuisine while strolling through the city's ancient streets.

Section 3: Best Times of Year to Take the Family on Adventure

3.1 Fall: September to November

Santiago de Compostela in the autumn is a different, but no less wonderful, experience for families. The weather is pleasant and temperate, with typical daytime highs of 15°C to 22°C (59°F to 72°F). The city is less busy.

Remarkable Occasions:

Explore the vibrant foliage found in the city's parks and gardens, which makes for a lovely setting for family portraits.
Let kids run free as you explore the Old Town's historic streets sans the throngs of summer visitors.
Take part in the family-friendly cultural events and activities of the San Froilán Festival in October.
3.2 Winter: From December to February

With fewer tourists, winter is the most serene and contemplative season in Santiago de Compostela. The typical daytime temperature is between 8°C and 15°C (46°F and 59°F).

Remarkable Occasions:

Savor traditional Galician cuisine and hot chocolate in neighborhood cafés to embrace the warm winter atmosphere.
During the slower months, visit the Santiago Cathedral and take in its tranquil ambiance.
Think of taking your family to explore the Camino de Santiago pilgrimage route and see the trail from a fresh perspective in the winter.
Section 4: Special Observations for the Family Camino de Santiago Trek

4.1 Autumn and Spring for Family Travel:

Spring and fall are perhaps the best seasons for families with young pilgrims to start the Camino de Santiago. The pleasant weather throughout these seasons is ideal for family outings and strolls.

Remarkable Occasions:

A special chance for family connection arises on the Camino, as you travel together, get to know other pilgrims, and enjoy the Galician scenery.
Kids should be encouraged to gather stamps, or sellos, along the Camino in order to make a memento of their journey.
Considerations for the Summer:

Even though summer is the busiest travel season for pilgrims traveling the Camino de Santiago, the heat makes it difficult. It's important for families with kids to be ready for warmer weather and maybe crowded lodgings.

Remarkable Occasions:

Kids are welcome to take part in the summertime events along the Camino, including pilgrimage meetings and cultural activities.

To provide a good experience and to meet the requirements of younger pilgrims, consider planning shorter daily walking lengths.

Section5: Concluding Thoughts for an Amazing Family Vacation

5.1 Modifications:

Make reservations for family-friendly lodging far in advance, regardless of the season, to guarantee that your loved ones will have everything they need. Seek for lodging options like flats or motels with amenities for kids.

5.2 Regional Foods:

Share the mouthwatering flavors of Galician food with your family. Try some classic fare like churros with hot chocolate, pulpo a la gallega (octopus), and empanadas.

5.3 Health and Safety:

Especially if your family is walking the Camino de Santiago, make sure they have access to the essential medical supplies and travel insurance.

Learn the emergency numbers and medical facilities in your area.

5.4 Immersion in Culture:

Through participating in festivals, experiencing customary pastimes, and mingling with amiable residents, you can encourage your kids to appreciate the local way of life.

Families and loved ones are cordially welcomed in Santiago de Compostela, which offers a wealth of family-friendly activities, cultural encounters, and breathtaking scenery for exploration. Whether your family prefers the lively atmosphere of summer, the brilliant splendor of autumn, the comfort of winter, or the revitalizing ambience of spring, there is no right or wrong time to come.

Santiago de Compostela guarantees a remarkable trip full of shared adventures and cultural discoveries, regardless of when you decide to travel there.

Chapter 11

Santiago de Compostela's Top Tourist Destinations You Must See and Booking Tips.

Galicia's capital, Santiago de Compostela, is a spiritual, cultural, and historical city in Spain. The main reason for its fame is that it is the last stop on the Camino de Santiago pilgrimage route. But the city has much more to offer than just religious significance. We will examine the main tourist sites in Santiago de Compostela in this extensive guide, along with advice on how to get there.

1. The Cathedral of Santiago de Compostela

Address: s/n Praza do Obradoiro

The Santiago de Compostela Cathedral, also known as just "the Cathedral," is the city's most recognizable and revered landmark. It is the last stop for pilgrims who have finished the Camino de Santiago and is where St. James's tomb is located.

Travel Advice:

Walking: The Cathedral is inherently reached by pilgrims traveling the Camino de Santiago.

Public Transportation: The bus system in Santiago is well-connected. Praza do Obradoiro, which is a short stroll from the Cathedral, may be reached by city bus.

Taxi: The Cathedral can be reached by taxi, which are widely available around the city.

Parking: There are garages and parking lots close to the Cathedral if you're driving, but get there early because they can get busy.

2. Quintana Plaza

The place is Quintana Plaza.

Plaza Quintana is a charming square that is next to the cathedral. Notable features include the Puerta Santa (Holy Door), which is only accessible during Jubilee years, and its historic structures.

Travel Advice:

Walking: The Old Town's main attractions, including the Cathedral, are all easily accessible on foot from the plaza.

Public Transportation: One easy method to get to Plaza Quintana is by bus, which stops at Praza do Obradoiro.

Guided Tours: To learn more about Plaza Quintana and its background, think about taking a guided walking tour of Santiago.

Pointe das Praterías 3.

The address is Praza das Praterías.

Santiago de Compostela also boasts another picturesque square, Praza das Praterías. The Fuente de los Caballos, a stunning fountain with horses on it, and the Casa del Cabildo, an outstanding 18th-century structure, are located there.

Travel Advice:

Walking: Praza das Praterías is a convenient place to explore on foot, just like many other Old Town sights in Santiago.

Public Transportation: The easiest way to get to Praza do Obradoiro is via city bus, which stops there.

4. Santiago's Abastos Market

Address: s/n Rúa das Ameas

Santiago's Mercado de Abastos is a thriving food market. Experience the authentic Galician cuisine and savor locally produced cheeses, artisanal goods, and fresh seafood.

Travel Advice:

Marching: The market is a short stroll from your lodging if you're in the Old Town.

Public Transportation: Buses stop close to the market. Praza de Abastos is the nearest bus stop.

5. The Alameda Park

Address: s/n Rúa das Ameas

Description: Offering breathtaking views of the city and the Cathedral, Parque de la Alameda is a lovely urban park. It's a peaceful haven where you can unwind and take in the scenery.

Travel Advice:

Walking: The Old Town and the Cathedral are both easily accessible on foot from the park.

Public Transportation: An easy way to get to the park is via the buses that travel through the city center.

Tours with a Guide: You might want to sign up for a walking tour with a guide that stops at Parque de la Alameda.

6. The Peregrinaciones Museum

Address: San Miguel dos Agros Rúa, s/n

The history of the Camino de Santiago and the pilgrims who have traveled to Santiago de Compostela over the ages are both celebrated in the Museum of Pilgrimages.

Travel Advice:

Walking: The museum is conveniently accessible on foot because it is situated in the Old Town.

Public Transportation: The museum can be easily accessed by bus, which travels through the city center.

7. Santiago's Abastos Market

Address: s/n Rúa das Ameas

Santiago's Mercado de Abastos is a thriving food market. Experience the authentic Galician cuisine and savor locally produced cheeses, artisanal goods, and fresh seafood.

Travel Advice:

Marching: The market is a short stroll from your lodging if you're in the Old Town.

Public Transportation: Buses stop close to the market. Praza de Abastos is the nearest bus stop.

8. La Casa Troya

Address: 7 Ría de San Paio de Antealtares

Santiago's historical Casa de la Troya is now a museum that offers insights into the city's past. It is an excellent example of a Galician home from the eighteenth century.

Travel Advice:

Walking: The museum is conveniently accessible on foot because it is situated in the Old Town.

Public Transportation: The museum can be easily accessed by bus, which travels through the city center.

Academia del Sar 9.

Place: Sar de Praza, s/n

The Colegiata del Sar is a rather remote Romanesque church from the city center. It is renowned for both its tranquil ambiance and stunning architecture.

Travel Advice:

Walking: Colegiata del Sar is reachable on foot, although it requires some hiking. Make sure your walking shoes are comfy.

Public Transportation: You can get to the church more easily via bus. At a tourist information center or the bus station, ask for directions.

Monte Pedroso, 10.

Where: The Monte Pedroso

Just outside of Santiago, on a hill called Monte Pedroso, are expansive vistas over the city and its environs. You can go hiking and have picnics there.

Travel Advice:

Walking: Depending on your pace, hiking Monte Pedroso can take one to two hours. The trailhead lies a bit beyond the city core.

Taxi: You can take a taxi to the foot of Monte Pedroso, where you can trek to reach the summit.

11. Center for Contemporary Art of Galicia (CGAC)

Address: s/n Ría Valle Inclán

The CGAC is a modern art museum that features Spanish and Galician art of the present day. It offers a distinctive contrast to the ancient landmarks of the city.

Travel Advice:

Walking: The museum is conveniently located in the heart of the city and is reachable by foot.

Public Transportation: The museum can be easily accessed by bus, which travels through the city center.

Parque da Belvís (addendum)

Location: s/n of Parque de Belvís

Parque da Belvís is a charming park with a view of Santiago de Compostela that is perched on a hill. With its verdant surroundings, strolling routes, and serene atmosphere, it's the ideal location to get away from the rush of the city.

Travel Advice:

Walking: From the Old Town, Parque da Belvís is reachable on foot, albeit with some hilly walking.

Public Transport: You can get reasonably close to the park by taking one of the buses that stop near the Old Town. You can walk there from there in a short amount of time.

Taxis: If you'd rather take a more direct path, taxis can drop you off at the park's entrance.

Tips for Making Reservations at the Best Tourist Attractions in Santiago de Compostela:

Plan Ahead: Santiago de Compostela is a well-liked travel destination, particularly in the summer when pilgrimages are at their highest. In order to guarantee admission to some sights (such guided tours or the Cathedral), it is best to make reservations well in advance, particularly if you have certain dates in mind.

Pilgrimage Lodging: It's imperative to reserve lodging in advance if you're walking the Camino de Santiago, particularly during popular seasons. Pilgrims can find plenty of albergues (hostels) and guesthouses, though availability may be restricted.

Guided Tours: If you want a more immersive and educational experience at different locations, think about taking one of the guided tours. Well-informed tour guides can enhance your experience by offering historical background.

Visits to Museums: Ahead of time, find out the museums' and cultural sites' admission fees and hours of operation. Certain museums might close for repairs on a given day or have shortened hours.

Transportation: Look into your choices for getting to sights that are a little outside of the city center, including Colegiata del Sar or Monte Pedroso, while making travel plans. Taxis, public transportation, and even rental bikes can work well for you, depending on your preferences.

Events and Festivals: Santiago holds a number of special events and festivals all year long, which may have an effect on the number of visitors and the availability of lodging. Make sure to reserve far in advance and organize your vacation appropriately if you wish to attend a specific festival.

Make Reservations for Meals: If you want to eat at a popular restaurant or one with a small seating capacity, you should think about doing so, especially during busy hours. This can help guarantee that you get a table at popular restaurants.

Language Skills: Although most people in Santiago de Compostela speak English, being able to communicate with locals will be easier if you know a little bit of basic Spanish or Galician. Think about picking up a few phrases or downloading a translation app.

Respect Local Customs: Dress modestly and abide by any applicable laws or customs when visiting places of worship, such as the Cathedral. Don't disrespect places that are holy.

Ticket Combos: A few attractions provide combo tickets that let you see several locations for less money. Look into these possibilities if you want to spend a day visiting a few different attractions.

Numerous historical, cultural, and ecological features in Santiago de Compostela appeal to a broad spectrum of interests. You can make the most of your trip to this fascinating city and guarantee that your exploration of its main tourist attractions is both memorable and enriching by carefully organizing your visit.

Santiago de Compostela Cathedral: A Guide to a Memorable Visit.

The "Catedral de Santiago," often known as the Santiago de Compostela Cathedral, is the spiritual pinnacle of the Camino de Santiago pilgrimage and the pulsating heart of the city. In addition to being a revered religious icon, this majestic cathedral is a work of architecture that draws tourists from all over the world. Along with some crucial booking advice, we'll go over the finest methods to visit the Santiago de Compostela Cathedral in this guide to make your visit genuinely unforgettable.

1. Arrange Your Visit Wisely

Especially during the busiest times of the year for pilgrimages and major religious occasions, the Santiago de Compostela Cathedral can get packed. In order to optimize your visit, take into account these tactical planning suggestions:

Timing: To escape the biggest crowds, try to arrive early in the morning or late in the afternoon. Typically, the Cathedral is accessible to guests from early in the morning until late at night.

Weekday Visits: Compared to weekends, weekday visits (Monday through Friday) are typically less crowded.

If at all feasible, schedule your visit during one of the Jubilee Years, which occur when July 25th, the Feast of St. James, falls on a Sunday. This is a unique and spiritually meaningful time to visit, as pilgrims receive a special indulgence throughout certain years.

2. In-depth Guided Tours

If you want to fully understand the Cathedral's spirituality, art, and history, you might want to take a guided tour. Insights and anecdotes from knowledgeable advisors can improve your experience:

Official Tours: There are multilingual guided tours available at the Cathedral. These excursions take you through the rooftop, which offers expansive views of the city, the crypt, and several chapels.

Private visits: These more individualized visits let you concentrate on certain facets of the Cathedral's history and architecture. They can be scheduled in advance.

3. The Mass of Pilgrims and Botafumeiro

For several tourists, one of the highlights is attending the Pilgrim's Mass at the Cathedral. To get the most out of this experience, follow these tips:

be There Early: To guarantee a seat at the Mass, arrive well in advance. The service might be busy. Priority seating is frequently granted to pilgrims who have completed the Camino de Santiago.

Botafumeiro: If you go to the Pilgrim's Mass, you may see the enormous incense burner known as the Botafumeiro swinging. Check the schedule for days when it's in operation because it's a rare sight.

4. Go Up to the Roof

The chance to tour the Santiago de Compostela Cathedral's rooftop, which offers expansive views of the city and the Praza do Obradoiro, is one of the most noteworthy features of the building:

Reserving a Rooftop Tour: A guided rooftop tour must be scheduled in advance in order to gain access to the rooftop. These small-group tours offer a fantastic overview of the Cathedral's architectural design.

5. Proper Clothes and Civil Conduct

Respecting the sacred setting and abiding by the dress rules are imperative when visiting the Santiago de Compostela Cathedral:

Wear attire that covers your knees and shoulders to demonstrate modesty. It's possible that exposing clothing, short skirts, and sleeveless tops are prohibited inside the cathedral.

Silence and Respect: When you're inside the cathedral, act with courtesy. It's a place of worship, where keeping quiet is frequently advised.

Organizing Advice for a Special Cathedral Visit:

Reservations for Tours: Make sure to book your rooftop visits and guided tours well in advance, particularly during the busiest travel times. These tours can be scheduled at the visitor center or on the Cathedral's official website.

Pilgrims' Priority: During the Pilgrim's Mass, if you are a pilgrim who has finished the Camino de Santiago, make use of your preferred seating. As proof, make sure you have your Pilgrim's Credential.

Online Tickets: If you want to avoid standing in line, especially for guided tours and entrance tickets, think about buying your tickets online in advance.

Respect Religious Events: If you intend to attend, make sure you are aware of the times and schedule of religious events. Recognize that during religious services, some locations might be off-limits to visitors.

Photography: While generally permitted, photography may be prohibited at Mass or in some other locations. Consider carefully where and when to shoot pictures.

Language: To guarantee that a guide who speaks your language is available if you would like a guided tour in a particular language, ask about language options when making your reservation.

A trip to the Santiago de Compostela Cathedral is memorable both culturally and spiritually. Through careful planning, participation in guided tours, and courteous conduct, you may fully immerse yourself in the rich history and artistic legacy of this remarkable house of worship, creating a truly unforgettable experience.

Plaza Quintana: Unveiling the Charm of Santiago de Compostela

Located in the center of Santiago de Compostela, Plaza Quintana is a historically significant, architecturally stunning, and vibrant area of the city. This charming area, which is frequently missed by visitors, provides a peaceful haven from the busy streets as well as a fascinating view into the rich history of the city. We'll go through the top strategies for visiting Plaza Quintana to make your trip genuinely unforgettable in this guide, along with some crucial booking advice.

1. Learn About the Past

Plaza Quintana is a historical location rather than merely a square. To get the most out of your trip, spend some time learning about its intriguing past:

Guided Tours: You might want to sign up for a walking tour that takes you through Plaza

Quintana. Skilled tour guides can share their thoughts about the surrounding architecture and the historical significance of the square.

Take a tour of the 18th-century Casa del Cabildo, which is situated on the eastern side of the square. The stunning façade serves as evidence of Santiago's rich architectural history.

2. The Holy Door, or Puerta Santa

The Santiago de Compostela Cathedral's Puerta Santa, or Holy Door, is one of Plaza Quintana's most striking features.

When the Feast of St. James (July 25th) falls on a Sunday, Jubilee Years are when the Puerta Santa is usually opened. Attending the Holy Door's opening ceremony if your visit falls within one of these exceptional years is an unforgettable experience.

Spiritual Significance: The Holy Door is a must-visit location because pilgrims who pass through it during a Jubilee Year are granted a special indulgence. If you're visiting the Cathedral, check the schedule to make sure the entry will be open.

3. Calm Ambience of Plaza Quintana

In contrast to some of Santiago's livelier squares, Plaza Quintana provides a calm environment that's ideal for unwinding:

Outdoor Seating: Take a seat at one of the quaint cafés encircling the area and enjoy a leisurely coffee or snack. It's a great place to people watch and take in the historic surroundings because it has outside seats.

Still Moments: The calm surroundings of Plaza Quintana provide a great setting for introspection. Settle down on a bench, pick up a book, or just enjoy the atmosphere.

Reservation Advice for an Exceptional Trip to Plaza Quintana:

Planning for a Jubilee Year: Make sure you book well in advance if your visit falls during one of these years. Larger crowds are to be expected during this time, particularly if you plan to enter through the Holy Door. Make sure you reserve your lodging in advance.

Guided Tours: If you want to learn more about the background and significance of Plaza Quintana, you should think about scheduling a guided tour. This square and other important attractions are covered on walking tours that are offered by a number of tour companies in Santiago.

El Cabildo Casa Hours: If you desire to tour the interior of the Casa del Cabildo, verify its opening hours in advance. Access to the building could be restricted, especially at certain periods of the year.

Outside Seating: Make a reservation if you want to eat or drink at one of the square's cafés, especially during the busiest travel seasons. The square is charming, which makes outdoor seating very popular.

Respect Local Customs: Although Plaza Quintana is a laid-back area, it's still necessary to show consideration for other guests and the surrounding area. Reduce your volume and make sure that any rubbish is disposed of properly.

Language Skills: Although most people in Santiago de Compostela speak English, being able to communicate with locals will be easier if you know a little bit of basic Spanish or Galician. Think about picking up a few phrases or downloading a translation app.

In Santiago de Compostela, Plaza Quintana is a hidden gem that provides a special fusion of tranquility, spirituality, and history. This picturesque area in the center of the city may make for an incredibly unforgettable experience if you explore its historical attractions, enjoy the atmosphere, and observe local customs.

Parque de la Alameda: Santiago's Green Oasis.

Located in the center of Santiago de Compostela, the charming urban park Parque de la Alameda is a tranquil sanctuary where luxuriant vegetation, ancient trees, and expansive vistas come together. This peaceful haven invites guests to relax, explore, and re-establish a connection with nature while providing a break from the busy streets of the city. We'll reveal the top strategies for visiting Parque de la Alameda for an incredibly unforgettable experience in this guide, along with crucial reservation advice.

1. Take in the Natural Beauty of the Park

Because of its many natural beauties, Parque de la Alameda is a must-visit location for individuals who love the outdoors and want to unwind. The following are some tips for taking in the park's breathtaking scenery:

Walking Trails: There are several well-kept walking trails winding through the park's lush vegetation, making it the ideal place for a brisk stroll or a revitalizing jog.

Botanical Variety: Look out for the park's varied vegetation, which includes old trees that are hundreds of years old, vibrant flowers, and even a quaint pond that is home to ducks. In order to preserve the park's unspoiled splendor, don't forget your camera.

2. Views of Santiago from Above

The magnificent panoramic view of Santiago de Compostela that Parque de la Alameda provides is one of its most notable characteristics. To fully enjoy this view:

Proceed to the Mirador de la Alameda, a vantage point located inside the park. Enjoy expansive views of the Santiago de Compostela Cathedral and the city's historic core from this location.

Sunset Spectacle: Time your visit to take in the Cathedral's golden glow as the sun sets. You won't quickly forget what you see.

3. Savor the Calm Environment

The tranquil environment of Parque de la Alameda is ideal for introspection and rest. Here's how you really enjoy the tranquil atmosphere of the park:

Carry a picnic basket and savor your food on any of the park's grassy patches or benches. It's the perfect approach to replenish yourself and enjoy the peace.

Reading Nooks: Grab a book, locate a peaceful area beneath a tree's shade, and immerse yourself in a good book. There are several quiet spots in the park where one can read.

How to Make Reservations for an Exceptional Trip to Parque de la Alameda:

Schedule: Although Parque de la Alameda is open all year round, its ambiance changes with the seasons. Vibrant colors and blossoms are brought by spring and early summer, while richly shaded foliage is seen in autumn. Think about the season that best suits your tastes.

Tours with a Guide: Although Parque de la Alameda does not require guided tours, you can combine a visit to the park with a walking tour guide of Santiago de Compostela. This enables you to take advantage of an experienced guide's insights while exploring a variety of places.

Sunset Visits: If you visit Parque de la Alameda in the late afternoon or early evening, you will be able to see the Cathedral lit up by the setting sun.

Planning Your Picnic: If you're going to have a picnic in the park, be sure to prepare your food ahead of time and pack any items you'll need, such cutlery and a blanket.

Respect the Environment: When taking in the natural beauty of the park, don't forget to dispose of any rubbish properly and don't disturb the animals.

Language Skills: Although most people in Santiago de Compostela speak English, being able to communicate with locals will be easier if you know a little bit of basic Spanish or Galician. Think about picking up a few phrases or downloading a translation app.

A tranquil diversion from Santiago de Compostela's bustle can be found in Parque de la Alameda. Whether you're enjoying a peaceful moment, exploring the park's lush surroundings, or taking in the breathtaking views, this urban sanctuary guarantees an unforgettable experience for guests of all ages.

Mercado de Abastos de Santiago: A Culinary Adventure in Galicia

The vibrant food market of Santiago de Compostela, Mercado de Abastos de Santiago, is a gourmet paradise that entices the senses with the tastes and scents of Galician cuisine. Discover a world of fresh, local fruit, seafood, cheeses, and more at this lively market, which is a food lover's heaven. Immerse yourself in the region's culinary traditions here. We'll go through the top strategies for visiting Mercado de Abastos for an absolutely amazing experience in this guide, along with some crucial booking advice.

1. Get there early for vibrancy and freshness

Take into account the following for the freshest and liveliest Mercado de Abastos experience:

Early Mornings: Get there early to see the market come to life with activity. There's a lot of enthusiasm in the air and the stalls are well stocked.

Weekdays: You may more easily explore the market at your own leisure on weekdays because they are usually less crowded than weekends, especially from Tuesday through Friday.

2. Discover the Market's Pleasures

Fresh ingredients and a variety of delicious delicacies are available at Mercado de Abastos. Here's how to maximize your time there:

Seafood Abounds: Galicia is renowned for its seafood, so don't miss the seafood stalls where you can sample a wide variety of fresh catches, like as clams, octopus, and salmon.

Cheese and Dairy: Savor some of the best cheeses and dairy products from Galicia. Try the local cheeses, such as San Simón and tetilla.

Local Produce: Take a look around the stands filled with vibrantly colored fruits, veggies, and fragrant herbs. Ripe tomatoes and peppers are examples of seasonal foods that are very tasty.

Savor the Traditions: Seek out food stands serving classic Galician fare such as savory pastries called empanadas, octopus prepared in the Gallega style, and pork with turnip greens called lacón con grelos. These foods offer a true flavor of the area.

3. Interact with the Suppliers

Engaging with the amiable merchants can improve your day at Mercado de Abastos:

Pose inquiries: Never be afraid to ask questions or get recommendations regarding the merchandise. Suppliers are frequently enthusiastic about what they have to offer and willing to impart their wisdom.

Examine the Goods: A lot of suppliers provide product samples. Enjoy the regional specialties and be willing to explore new flavors.

Discover Local food Advice: Talk to sellers to find out about customs and recipes related to traditional Galician food. You may learn some insightful culinary tidbits.

How to Make Reservations for an Exceptional Trip to Mercado de Abastos:

Timing: For the freshest options and a bustling ambiance, try to visit the market early in the morning. Weekdays are recommended over weekends if you want a more sedate atmosphere.

Photography: While it's generally acceptable to take pictures, please consider the privacy and comfort of the sellers and other customers. Permission is always required if you want to take a picture of a seller.

Cash and Cards: Since some stalls might not take credit or debit cards, bring both cash and cards. It guarantees you can buy the things you want if you have a range of payment choices.

Shopping Bags: If you intend to buy fresh vegetables or other products, think about packing a reusable shopping bag or tote to carry your purchases.

Local Currency: For transactions within the market, use the local currency, which is euros. If necessary, there are currency exchange facilities in Santiago de Compostela.

Language Proficiency: Although a lot of merchants might speak basic English, being able to communicate in Spanish or Galician can improve your experience in general.

Discover the rich culinary traditions of Galicia and indulge in the region's delectable flavors at Mercado de Abastos de Santiago, a veritable culinary treasure trove. By coming early, perusing the market's many goods, interacting with merchants, and paying attention to reservation guidelines, you may enjoy the culinary treats of this lively marketplace and create a genuinely unforgettable experience.

Praza das Praterías: Where History and Beauty Converge

Discover the hidden jewel of Praza das Praterías, a lovely area tucked away in the ancient center of Santiago de Compostela. In honor of the silversmiths (prateiros) who formerly worked here, this charming square bears their name. Visitors are enthralled with Praza das Praterías due to its sophisticated architecture, historical significance, and lively atmosphere. We'll share our top recommendations for visiting Praza das Praterías for an unforgettable experience along with crucial booking advice in this guide.

Examine the Magnificence of Architecture

Praza das Praterías is well known for its historic structures and stunning architecture. To totally understand its allure, think about these investigative suggestions:

Casa del Cabildo: Take a closer look at this neoclassical, eighteenth-century structure to start your tour. Its magnificent façade, which is embellished with sculptures and minute details, is evidence of Santiago's rich architectural history.

Fuente de los Caballos: Take in the stunning scenery of this fountain, which is adorned with statues of horses. The area gains a hint of refinement from its elaborate fountain.

2. Learn about the Paradise Gate, or Puerta del Paraíso.

The Puerta del Paraíso, or Paradise Gate, which leads to Santiago de Compostela Cathedral, is one of Praza das Praterías' most notable features. How to maximize this historic feature is as follows:

Historical Significance: The major entryway for pilgrims who finish the Camino de Santiago is the Puerta del Paraíso. It provides a window into pilgrims' spiritual journeys and is full of symbolism.

Exquisite Detailing: Give the gate's elaborate carvings and sculptures some thought. Every component adds to the artistic and historical significance of the gate and tells a tale.

3. Enjoy the Liveliness of the Square

Beyond only being a historical place, Praza das Praterías is a hive of activity. To take in the vibrant atmosphere of the square:

Outside Cafés: Stop by one of the outside cafés around the square for a meal or a cup of coffee. It's a great place to observe people and take in the local culture.

Street Performers: Depending on the time of day, the square may be attended by musicians or street performers who bring a little entertainment value.

How to Make Reservations for an Exceptional Trip to Praza das Praterías?

Date of Access: Praza das Praterías is open all year round. Try going in the early morning or late afternoon to escape the big crowds. Weekends tend to be busier than weekdays.

Tours Guided: Although you don't need a guide to see the square itself, you might want to sign up for a walking tour of Santiago de Compostela. This gives you the opportunity to see Praza das Praterías and other historical monuments while learning insightful things from an experienced guide.

Hours of the Casa del Cabildo: If you intend to tour the inside, make sure to confirm the hours of operation beforehand. Access may be restricted, particularly during particular seasons of the year.

Language Skills: Although most people in Santiago de Compostela speak English, being able to communicate with locals will be easier if you know a little bit of basic Spanish or

Galician. Think about picking up a few phrases or downloading a translation app.

Behaving Respectfully: Keep in mind to show consideration for the surrounding area, other guests, and any ongoing events or performances while you take in the beauty and ambiance of the plaza.

Praza das Praterías is a charming square with historical value, elegant architecture, and a vibrant atmosphere. Basking in the timeless appeal of this hidden jewel within Santiago de Compostela, you may make your stay truly unforgettable by discovering its architectural gems, admiring the Puerta del Paraíso, and taking in the lively atmosphere of the square.

Parque de la Alameda: Santiago's Scenic Oasis

Located in the center of Santiago de Compostela, Parque de la Alameda is a verdant urban oasis that provides a calm diversion from the bustle of the city with its peaceful strolling trails, thick vegetation, and breathtaking views. This vast park is a haven for both residents and tourists, beckoning everyone to rest, commune with the natural world, and take in the sweeping vistas of Santiago. We'll reveal the top strategies for visiting Parque de la Alameda for an incredibly unforgettable experience in this guide, along with crucial reservation advice.

1. When to Make the Ideal Visit

distinct times of the day and year bring distinct lights to Parque de la Alameda. Here's how to maximize your time there:

Morning strolls: Take a stroll in the park first thing in the morning to take in the peaceful atmosphere and the cool dew on the grass.

Golden Hour: Come in the late afternoon to take in the Cathedral and the city's enchanting glow as the sun sets, bathing everything in warm, golden tones.

Seasonal Blooms: Autumn paints the park in gold and scarlet tones, while spring delivers vibrant flowers. Take into account your preferred season for a truly unforgettable encounter.

2. Breathtaking Scenes and Views

Parque de la Alameda is the ideal location for leisure and photography because it provides stunning views of Santiago:

Visit the Mirador de la Alameda, a parkvista located inside the area. Enjoy expansive vistas of Santiago's historic district and the famous

Santiago de Compostela Cathedral from this location.

Pond and Fountain: Take a stroll around the park's quaint pond and fountain area, which is a peaceful place to sit, read a book, or just take in the peaceful atmosphere.

3. Recreation and Nature

The park's recreational options and scenic surroundings guarantee an enjoyable visit:

Walking & Jogging: Take a leisurely stroll or a revitalizing jog along the park's well-kept walking paths.

Carry a picnic basket and enjoy your meal on a park bench or on an open patch of grass. It's a great way to relax and get back in touch with nature.

How to Make Reservations for an Exceptional Trip to Parque de la Alameda:

Transport: Due to its strategic location in Santiago's downtown, Parque de la Alameda is easily reachable on foot from the majority of the city's districts. Public transportation is also an option; city buses can drop you off close by.

Tours Guided: Although tours are not required in the park, you might want to sign up for one of Santiago de Compostela's walking tours, which include a stop at Parque de la Alameda. Guides frequently share anecdotes and historical context regarding the significance of the park.

Sunset Spectacle: If you visit Parque de la Alameda in the late afternoon or early evening, you can see the Cathedral illuminated by the golden light of sunset.

Planning a Picnic: If you're having a picnic at the park, don't forget to pack cutlery, a blanket, and your favorite snacks. The park does not have any food options.

Behaving Respectfully: Keep in mind to show consideration for the surrounding area and other guests as you take in the natural beauty of the park. Please dispose of waste properly.

Language Skills: Although most people in Santiago de Compostela speak English, being able to communicate with locals will be easier if you know a little bit of basic Spanish or Galician. Think about picking up a few phrases or downloading a translation app.

A calm urban haven, Parque de la Alameda offers sweeping views of Santiago, opportunities to engage with the city's past, and the beauty of nature. You may immerse yourself in this verdant sanctuary in the center of Santiago de Compostela and create a genuinely unforgettable vacation by picking the ideal time to visit, exploring picturesque areas, and appreciating the park's peacefulness.

Santiago de Compostela's Scenic Sit-Out Points: A Haven for Recreation.

Located in the heart of Galicia, Spain, Santiago de Compostela is a city rich in history and culture as well as a site where the splendor of the natural world blends harmoniously with city life. Discovering the city's picturesque sit-out spots is a great way to take in the natural beauty and lively vibe of Santiago. We shall explore some of Santiago de Compostela's top sit-out locations for leisure in this thorough tour.

Alameda Park: An Eco-Friendly Sanctuary in the Center of the City

Location: Alameda Road

A beautiful urban park called Alameda Park may be found right in the center of Santiago. Encompassing an area of 8 hectares, it provides a tranquil haven away from the busy streets. Its arched entrance welcomes you with a plethora of plants, fountains, and statues. The park's design offers a range of areas for leisure thanks to a flawless fusion of French and English garden traditions.

What's Next:

Choose a grassy area or bench to read, have a picnic, or just take in the tranquil surroundings.

Discover the park's botanical garden, which has a variety of plant types.

See the Dos Galos Fountain, a well-liked gathering spot and city emblem.

2. The Panoramic Peak of Monte Pedroso

Location: Northwest of Santiago; bus or hiking trail can get you there.

The best place for someone looking for a little adventure is Monte Pedroso. A broad perspective of Santiago and its environs may be seen from this little peak. You may reach the summit after a 2.5-kilometer climb from the city center, where you'll be treated to breath-taking views.

What's Next:

Climb to the summit for a breathtaking view of the sun coming up or setting.

Sack up and have a picnic while taking in the scenery.

Explore the little hermitage at the top and take in the peaceful atmosphere.

3. The Historical and Scenic Beauty of Belvís Park

Place: Calle de San Pedro

Beside the Belvís Convent, Belvís Park is a lovely green area that blends natural beauty with historical charm. With its views of the city and tree-lined roads, it's the perfect spot for a leisurely stroll.

What's Next:

Discover the history of the Belvís Convent by paying it a visit.

Investigate the elaborate fountains and sculptures throughout the park.

Take a seat on one of the benches and enjoy the quiet atmosphere.

4. Rooftop Patios: Drinks and City Views

In Santiago, there are a number of establishments with rooftop terraces that provide some of the most breathtaking city views. Though not your typical places to sit outside, these terraces offer an opulent way to relax and take in the city views.

What's Next:

In one of the rooftop bars, take a cocktail or savor a meal while taking in the scenery.

As the sun sets, take in the beauty of the city via the lens of your camera.

5. Parque de Bonaval: A Sanctuary of Culture

Place: Calle de Bonaval

Parque de Bonaval is a center of culture as well as a park. Located next to the Museo do Pobo Galego (Galician People's Museum) and the Santo Domingo de Bonaval Church, this park provides a calm setting for taking in the scenery and artistic creations.

What's Next:

Investigate the various artworks and sculptures positioned across the park.

Attend concerts and cultural events hosted at the amphitheater of the park.

For a comprehensive experience, pair your visit with a visit to the Galician People's Museum.

6. Paseo da Ferradura: Unwind by the Riverside

Location: Close to the Old Town, along the Sar River

The charming promenade along the river, Paseo da Ferradura, offers a tranquil diversion from the activity of the city. The Sar River winds along the tree-lined walkway, which provides peace and quiet in the middle of the city.

What's Next:

Enjoy the shade of the trees as you wander slowly down the river.

Take a seat on the riverbank with a book and enjoy the soothing sound of the running water.

Seize the city's reflections in the river to create memorable images.

7. Eugenio Granell Park: Art and Nature Collide

Place: Valle del Río Inclán

In Parque Eugenio Granell, which bears the name of the well-known surrealist painter from Galicia, art and environment cohabit together. For those looking for a more creative and reflective experience, it's a tranquil haven.

What's Next:

Take in the park's sculptures and art pieces.

Visit the cultural hub of the park to take in the art exhibits and events.

Look for a shady area where you can paint or draw the lovely surroundings.

San Domingos de Bonaval Viewpoint: An Undiscovered Treasure

Location: next to the church of Santo Domingo de Bonaval

With the Cathedral serving as the main feature, this less well-known vantage point provides a distinctive view of Santiago's skyline. You may take in the splendor of the city without the crowds at this serene location.

What's Next:

Take breathtaking pictures of the Cathedral with the rich vegetation framing it.

Admire the city's historic center while indulging in a peaceful moment of contemplation.

Take some time to explore the Santo Domingo de Bonaval Church, which is close by.

9. Mirador do Cervo: A Beautiful View

Where: Ría Tras Salomé

A hidden treasure in Santiago de Compostela is Mirador do Cervo. Though it's a little off the usual route, it provides striking views of the city from an unusual vantage point.

What's Next:

Take in expansive views of Santiago, which include the Alameda Park and the Cathedral.

Take a seat on one of the stone benches and enjoy the tranquil atmosphere.

Discover the city's charming charms by strolling around the surrounding streets.

10. A Bright Square in Plaza Cervantes

Place: Cervantes Road

Plaza Cervantes is a bustling square where you can take in the surrounding architecture and flora and feel the vibe of the community.

What's Next:

Enjoy a cappuccino or a freshly baked croissant while sitting at one of the outdoor cafes.

Enjoy people watching as visitors and residents interact in this lively square.

Discover the neighboring streets for dining and shopping, such as Rúa de Cervantes.

The picturesque sit-out spots in Santiago de Compostela provide a beautiful fusion of urban charm, natural beauty, and history. Whether you're looking for peace & quiet, cultural encounters, or just somewhere to relax and take in the beauty of the city, these places offer the ideal environment for leisure and relaxation. You'll learn the real spirit of Santiago de

Compostela if you take your time discovering these undiscovered treasures.

Chapter 12

Outdoors Activities in Santiago de Compostela.

Travelers looking to get in touch with nature, history, and culture will find a wonderful selection of outdoor activities available in Santiago de Compostela, which is tucked away in the scenic Galician area of northwest Spain. As the last stop on the Camino de Santiago pilgrimage, the city is well-known for its spiritual significance, but it is also a paradise for outdoor aficionados. We will examine the various outdoor experiences Santiago de Compostela provides in this extensive guide, including trekking the Camino pathways, exploring verdant parks and gardens, and engaging in adventurous activities.

Section 1: A Tour of the Santiago Camino

1.1 Hiking the Camino of Santiago:

The Camino de Santiago, a system of pilgrimage paths that leads to Santiago de Compostela, is often associated with the city. Start an adventure to remember by trekking a section of the Camino. You'll pass through picturesque scenery, quaint villages, and historic attractions whether you take the French Way, the Portuguese Way, or an other path.

Passport for Pilgrims (Credencial del Peregrino):

Obtain a Pilgrim's Passport (Credencial del Peregrino) if you plan to walk part of the Camino. Along the way, it provides admission to albergues and pilgrim hostels, in addition to acting as a memento.

1.3 Arrival at Santiago Cathedral:

Walk to Santiago de Compostela to feel the triumph that pilgrims have felt for generations. Get a Compostela certificate at the Santiago Cathedral by participating in the Pilgrim's Mass, which attests to your pilgrimage.

Section 2: Parks and Natural Retreats

2.1 Park Alameda:

One of Santiago's most famous parks, Alameda Park, is a great place to start your exploration of the city's green areas. Explore exquisitely designed gardens, take in historically significant statues, and relax on the park's terraces to take in expansive city views.

2.2 The Bonaval Park:

In close proximity to the Santiago Cathedral sits the tranquil and artistic haven known as Parque de Bonaval. Discover its peaceful gardens, artistic creations, and the wacky Tree of Love, which has come to represent the park.

2.3 Pedroso de Montes:

Hike up the city's famous hill, Monte Pedroso, for a more strenuous outdoor experience. Gaining access to the summit will reward you with amazing vistas of Santiago and the surroundings.

2.4 Rocha Forte Park:

This historic park has the remains of a medieval stronghold, as well as beautiful ponds and lush gardens. It's a great place for a family picnic, leisurely stroll, and birdwatching.

Section Three: River Experiences

3.1 Trail Rio Sarela:

Take a leisurely stroll along the Río Sarela route, which passes through verdant vegetation and provides views of Santiago's breathtaking natural surroundings.

3.2.2 Ulla River Kayaking:

Kayaking on the Ulla River, which meanders through the Galician countryside, is a thrilling option for anyone seeking adventure. All skill levels can enjoy guided kayaking experiences offered by a number of tour operators in Santiago.

Section 4: Outdoor Sports and Adventure

4.1 Paths for Biking:

Hire a bicycle to go about Santiago and its environs on two wheels. Bike enthusiasts of all skill levels can enjoy the city's many bike trails and picturesque routes.

4.2 Playing Golf in Santiago's Real Aero Club:

Golfers can start their round at the scenic Real Aero Club de Santiago, which is only a short drive from the city center. The Galician countryside is breathtakingly visible from the course.

4.3 Gliding on air:

Take into consideration paragliding over the Galician countryside if you're an adrenaline junkie. This exhilarating activity provides a distinctive viewpoint of the local landscapes.

Section 5: Outdoor Cultural and Historic Sites

Castro de Elviña (5.1):

Explore the pre-Roman hillfort Castro de Elviña, which offers insights into the region's Celtic past. Discover the archaeological site while taking in the expansive vistas from the hilltop.

5.2 Trasouto de San Lorenzo:

Explore San Lorenzo de Trasouto, a charming village west of Santiago, and its ancient charms. Its church and typical Galician architecture are striking.

Section 6: Santiago Day Trips

6.1 Baixas Rías:

Go outside of Santiago and discover the breathtaking Rías Baixas region, renowned for its white-sand beaches, scenic coastline, and mouthwatering seafood. Explore the quaint village of Combarro and sample the Albariño wine produced in the Salnés Valley vineyards.

6.2 Muxía and Fisterra:

Take a day trip to Fisterra (Finisterre) and Muxía, two coastal towns that provide amazing vistas of the Atlantic Ocean and a feeling of pilgrimage completion, to continue your Camino journey.

Part 7: Regional Marketplaces

7.1 Santiago Market, or Mercado de Abastos de Santiago:

Visit the Mercado de Abastos to get a taste of Santiago's culinary culture. Residents and tourists alike congregate at this lively market to indulge in the finest Galician produce, seafood, cheeses, and other delicacies. Wander around the stalls, chat with the amiable traders, and enjoy typical Galician and Spanish cuisine at the market's restaurants.

7.2 Antiques and Crafts Fair, Feria de Antigüidades y Artesanía:

Be sure not to miss the Feria de Antigüedades y Artesanía if you have a fondness for antiques and handcrafted goods. This outdoor market in Santiago's Old Town is held on select weekends and offers a plethora of unusual treasures, such as vintage goods, artwork, and handcrafted goods.

7.3 The Organic Products Fair, or Feria de Productos Ecológicos:

A must-see for everyone interested in organic and sustainable products is the Feria de Productos Ecológicos. This market features handcrafted items, organic foods that are locally sourced, and environmentally friendly products. This is a fantastic chance to meet local producers and encourage eco-friendly practices.

Accepting Nature Discovery in Santiago

Adventurers of all ages and interests can enjoy the wide variety of outdoor activities offered by Santiago de Compostela. Santiago has plenty to offer outdoor enthusiasts, whether their passion is trekking the Camino de Santiago, discovering verdant parks and gardens, seeking adventure in the Galician countryside, or learning about the rich history and culture of the city. These encounters provide you the chance to not only interact with the area's natural beauty and heritage, but they also help you make lifelong memories of your trip to this charming city. Put on your walking shoes, bring your sense of adventure, and enjoy Santiago de Compostela's natural surroundings.

Santiago de Compostela Indoors: Culture, Art, and Leisure.

Although the Santiago Cathedral and the Camino de Santiago are two of the city's most well-known outdoor attractions, Santiago de Compostela also has a wide range of inside activities to offer people who are interested in culture, the arts, and leisure. Santiago de Compostela offers many of indoor activities, whether your goal is to take in the bustling cultural scene, learn about the city's past, or just get away from the occasional downpour. We will explore a wide range of indoor activities in this extensive guide to keep you occupied and amused while visiting this quaint Spanish city.

Section 1: Cultural Centers and Museums

1.1 Pilgrimage Museum, Museo de las Peregrinaciones:

Start your interior exploration at the Camino de Santiago historical museum, Museo de las

Peregrinaciones. These exhibits, which feature historical narratives, artwork, and artifacts, provide insights on the pilgrim's journey.

1.2 The Galician People's Museum, or Museo do Pobo Galego:

Visit the Museo do Pobo Galego to gain a deeper understanding of Galician tradition and culture. It offers a fascinating look into the past of the area with its vast collection of Galician folk art, clothing, tools, and customs.

1.3 Galician Center for Contemporary Art (Centro Galego de Arte Contemporánea, or CGAC):

For those who appreciate modern art, a visit to the CGAC is an absolute must. Modern and contemporary artworks by Spanish and international artists are displayed there in a rotating selection. Events, workshops, and exhibitions are also held at the facility.

Section 2: Architectural and Historical Treasures

2.1 Interior of Santiago Cathedral:

Don't miss the opportunity to tour the Santiago Cathedral's inside, even though its exterior is breathtaking. Admire the elaborate chapels, altarpieces, and the crypt, which is thought to contain Saint James's relics. The cathedral's museum is home to an extensive collection of holy artifacts.

2.2 Dos Reis Católicos Hostal:

Enter the storied Hostal dos Reis Católicos, a posh parador that was formerly a pilgrims' hospital. Its dining halls, salons, and elaborate cloister provide a window into the splendor of earlier times.

2.3 San Francisco Convent, often known as Convento de San Francisco:

The stunning cloister and calm interior of the Convento de San Francisco offer a peaceful respite from the bustle of the city. Admire the architectural intricacies of this historic landmark while strolling through its serene gardens.

Theaters and Performing Arts in Section Three

3.1 The Principal Theater, or Teatro Principal:

Experience a cultural evening in Santiago's oldest theater, Teatro Principal. For those who enjoy the arts, it offers a fascinating array of performances, such as opera, ballet, theater, and musical concerts.

3.2 Galicia Auditorium, or Auditorio de Galicia:

Our contemporary cultural complex serves as a center for performing arts. See the schedule for plays, concerts, dance classes, and other events. Artists and ensembles with international reputation frequently perform in the Auditorio de Galicia.

Section 4: Bookstores and Libraries

4.1 Galician Library (Biblioteca de Galicia):

Spend some time visiting the Biblioteca de Galicia, a wealth of information about Galician literature and history, if you're a bookworm. It also provides a peaceful area for reading and research, as well as housing temporary exhibitions.

4.2 The Cronopios Bookstore, or Librería Cronopios:

Investigate the quaint Librería Cronopios, a well-liked little bookshop offering a large assortment of books in many languages. It's a great site to look for your next book and find works by Galician authors.

Section 5: Culinary Adventures

5.1 Courses on Cooking:

Take a cooking class to really immerse yourself in Galician cuisine. Many locations provide interactive experiences where you can learn how to make local delicacies like empanadas and pulpo a la gallega (octopus).

5.2 Sommeliering:

Albariño and Ribeiro are two of Galicia's most well-known wines. Take a wine tasting at a nearby bodega or wine bar. Discover the methods used in the region's winemaking and sample its best vintages.

Section 6: Retreats for Spa and Wellness

6.1 Thermal and Spa Baths:

Visit a spa or thermal bath facility in Santiago de Compostela to indulge in relaxation and renewal. Take advantage of a variety of services, such as massages and thermal pools, that are meant to help you relax and feel refreshed.

Section 7: Retail Therapy and Shopping

7.1 Santiago Market, or Mercado de Abastos de Santiago:

Investigate the Santiago Market to learn more about the lively local way of life. You may taste fresh fruit, cheeses, seafood, and handcrafted goods at this lively indoor market. Talking with sellers and sampling regional cuisine is a unique experience.

7.2 Rúas Felipe and Nova:

Charming boutiques, shops, and gift shops adorn these old streets. It's the perfect location to purchase jewelry, linens, pottery, and traditional Galician crafts.

Section 8: Workshops for Education

8.1 Workshops for Arts and Crafts:

Take use of your creative side by attending workshops for crafts and art. Take up a traditional Galician craft like weaving baskets or pottery, or study modern art methods with the help of regional artists.

Section 9: Instruction in Language and Culture

9.1 Language Classes in Spanish or Galician:

Become fully immersed in the culture of the area by taking Spanish or Galician language courses. Gaining proficiency in the language makes traveling there more enriching and improves your comprehension of the local way of life.

Santiago's Cozy Interiors

The indoor activities in Santiago de Compostela provide a fun contrast to the city's outside attractions. Whether you're drawn to the city's culinary delights, wellness offers, or cultural treasures, there are a plethora of indoor activities that will stimulate your senses and mind. These encounters help you develop a deeper appreciation for Santiago's colorful culture, lengthy history, and friendly people, making your trip to this amazing city both educational and entertaining.

Chapter 13

Dining and entertainment.
The Best Options For Dining and Entertainment Restaurants in Santiago de Compostela with NightLife.

The capital of Galicia, in northwest Spain, Santiago de Compostela, is well-known for its thriving food scene and exciting nightlife in addition to its spiritual significance as the Camino de Santiago pilgrimage's ultimate destination. We will examine the top choices for nightlife, entertainment, and food in this historic city in our extensive guide.

Meals Options

There are many different dining alternatives in Santiago de Compostela, ranging from cosmopolitan food to traditional Galician cuisine. Here are a few highly suggested items:

The Soul of Galician Food at Casa Sindo

Place: 17 Rúa Nova

Food: Galician

Highlights: Known for its authentic Galician cuisine, Casa Sindo is a family-run restaurant. Savour the delicious "Pulpo a la Gallega" - octopus prepared in the Galician style - and the "Tarta de Santiago" dessert.

Dine with a Michelin Star at Culler de Pau

Address: 4 Rúa Travesa

Modern Galician cuisine

Highlights: Culler de Pau is a modern take on Galician cuisine and a Michelin-starred restaurant. The tasting menu takes you on a gourmet tour of Galician delicacies.

Fusion Delights: O Dezaseis

Address: 16 Rúa do Vilar

Cuisine: Blending

Highlights: O Dezaseis combines elements from Spain with other cultures. Creative delicacies like "Codfish Miso" and "Lacón with Teriyaki Sauce" are available on the menu.

Altamira Café: Traditional Spanish

Place: 6 Praza de Quintana

Food: Spanish

Remarkables: The menu at Café de Altamira consists of traditional Spanish cuisine, and the restaurant has a warm ambiance. The "Gazpacho" and "Paella" are definitely must-tries.

Enxebre Restaurant: Cozy Charm

The address is 9 Rúa de San Miguel dos Agros.

Food: Galician

Highlights: Traditional Galician cuisine and the rustic charm of Restaurante Enxebre are its specialties. Make sure not to miss "Empanada Gallega."

Outdoor Dining

The favorable temperature of Santiago de Compostela makes alfresco dining a pleasure. Here are some excellent locations for outdoor dining:

Plaza de Quintana: Adjacent to the Cathedral, this area is flanked by quaint eateries that provide alfresco dining. The location is perfect for people watching while dining.

Parque de Alameda: This lovely park provides a calm environment for outdoor meals and picnics.

Grab some regional specialties and savor them while surrounded by greenery.

Rúa do Franco: This bustling street has a sidewalk-lined frontage of eateries and bars. Take a seat outside and enjoy the local wines and snacks.

Authentic Recipes

The famous dish Pulpo a la Gallega is made with soft octopus that has been seasoned with salt, olive oil, and paprika. It's a classic Galician dish that most eateries serve.

The Empanada Gallega is a flaky pastry-wrapped savory pie filled with items such as cod, pork, or tuna. It's the ideal appetizer or snack.

Tarta de Santiago: A popular dish in Galicia, this is an almond cake. Usually, a powdered sugar dusting and the Saint James cross are applied.

Nightlife and Entertainment

Santiago de Compostela comes alive with a bustling entertainment scene and a variety of evening alternatives after a filling supper. Here's a little peek at what to anticipate:

Traditional Music at Tabernas: Live performances of traditional Galician music, including bagpipes and tambourines, are available at many tabernas and pubs. "A Casa das Crechas" and other similar locations frequently host these events.

Café & Jazz: For a more relaxed evening, check out Café Jazz Naima, where you can take in live jazz performances in a small venue.

Dancing till dawn is possible in Santiago's many nightclubs and discos, such as Moon Disco Club and Capitol, which play a variety of musical styles.

If you're feeling lucky, stop into Casino Cirsa Santiago for some entertainment and gaming. It provides a selection of table games and slot machines.

Theater and Performances: For information about upcoming plays, concerts, and other events, see the schedules at Teatro Principal and Auditorio de Galicia.

Nightlife Destinations

Rúa do Franco: This street contains late-night taverns and pubs in addition to restaurants. It's a fantastic spot to begin your evening.

Rúa de San Pedro: This street attracts a varied clientele and provides a vibrant atmosphere due to its unique blend of taverns and clubs.

Plaza de Cervantes: This area, which is close to the Cathedral, features patios and bars where you may sip drinks and take in the surrounding historic architecture.

Rúa da Raíña: Its vibrant nightlife scene makes this street popular with both locals and tourists. It is home to several trendy bars.

In addition to its spiritual importance, Santiago de Compostela is a place that satisfies the senses with its delectable cuisine and provides plenty of entertainment opportunities. Every traveler looking for an unforgettable experience in the heart of Galicia may find something to enjoy in Santiago, from indulging in traditional Galician cuisine to dancing the night away in its vibrant clubs.

Chapter 14

Hidden Gems: Neighborhood Exploration in Santiago de Compostela - Uncovering Treasures Off the Beaten Path.

Santiago de Compostela is a city well-known for its magnificent architecture, spiritual significance, and extensive history. The Santiago Cathedral and the Old Town are two of the city's most well-known sights, but there are a ton of other hidden treasures tucked away in the city's districts, just waiting for the inquisitive visitor to find them. We will take you on a tour to discover Santiago de Compostela's hidden pearls in this illustrative guide—the less well-known areas and hidden gems that showcase the city's distinct personality and charm.

Section 1: San Pedro's Barrio

1.1 Summary:

A neighborhood that frequently eludes the attention of ordinary tourists is Barrio de San Pedro. Nestled in the southwest corner of the city, it provides a tranquil and genuine sense of Santiago.

Hidden Treasures:

San Paio de Antealtares Convento:

Tucked beneath a modest façade, this little tenth-century convent is full of charm. Its tranquil courtyard and antique interior offer a calm diversion from the busy metropolis.

House of the Crechas:

a cultural hub that holds live music performances, workshops, and art exhibits. It's a great spot to get involved with the community's artistic scene.

San Paio Plaza:

A charming square with patio furniture that is bordered by charming eateries and cafes. It's a great place to enjoy a coffee and observe the passing scenery.

Section 2: San Roque Barrio

2.1 Summary:

The neighborhood of Barrio de San Roque is located east of the Old Town and has a laid-back vibe. Its little squares and winding streets are perfect for leisurely strolling.

2.2 Spotted Jewels:

The Bonaval Park:

a calm park that was once a cemetery, complete with sculptures, rich vegetation, and expansive city vistas. This serene haven is ideal for a leisurely walk.

The Pobo Galego Museum:

With displays of traditional art, tools, and costumes, this folk museum offers insights into Galician customs and culture.

Carmen O. Taberna:

A warm and inviting traditional Galician taverna where you may enjoy local wines and meals in an inviting setting.

Section 3: Belvís neighborhood

3.1 Summary:

Located south of the Old Town, Barrio de Belvís offers a blend of local life, greenery, and history. Visitors are frequently taken aback by this neighborhood's hidden gems.

3.2 Covert Jewels:

The Belvís Park:

a peaceful park featuring gardens, walkways, and breathtaking city views. It's the perfect location for a leisurely family picnic.

Santa María do Camiño Igrexa:

This quaint chapel has a serene interior and an amazing rose window. It is worthwhile to explore this hidden architectural gem.

Tertulia Café:

a charming café renowned for its literary heritage and cozy atmosphere. Sip coffee and take in the culture of the area.

Section 4: Sar's Barrios

4.1 Synopsis:

Southeast of the Old Town lies a residential neighborhood called Barrio de Sar, which has a thriving local scene. It provides a genuine window into the day-to-day activities of Santiago de Compostela.

4.2 Secret Treasures:

Santiago's Abastos Market:

This vibrant food market is less frequented by visitors, despite being somewhat concealed. Take a look at its stands offering cheeses, seafood, fresh veggies, and regional specialties.

Eugenio Granell Park:

a lovely park bearing the name Eugenio Granell, surrealist artist. It has grassy areas, playgrounds, and sculptures that are ideal for family outings.
A Curuxa Taberna:

a typical Galician pub well-known for its tapas and native cuisine. It's a wonderful location to experience regional flavors in a genuine atmosphere.
Section 5: Santa Marta Neighborhood

5.1 Synopsis:

Situated to the west of the Old Town, Barrio de Santa Marta presents a blend of historical landmarks and indigenous customs. Travelers that are curious can find hidden jewels in this neighborhood.
Enchanted Secrets:

Santa Marta Igrexa:

The interior of this 12th-century church is decorated with elaborate altars and holy artwork, and it has a stunning façade with Romanesque elements.

House of Troia:

a historic home turned museum offering an insight into Santiago's mediaeval history. Examine its well preserved chambers and antiques.

Do Real Forno:

an establishment that is well-known for its empanadas and other typical Galician pastries. It is a lovely location to enjoy real delicacies.

Section 6: Perspectives on Culture

6.1 Intimate Relationships:

A delightful aspect of discovering hidden neighborhoods is the chance to engage with the local population. Feel free to start a discussion, seek advice, or just take in the day-to-day activities in these less visited locations.

6.2 Celebrations and Occasions:

Look out for any festivals or other events that may be taking place in these neighborhoods. They frequently offer opportunities to partake in distinctive cultural experiences and rejoice with the people.

Beyond the city's well-known attractions, Santiago de Compostela's secret neighborhoods have a wealth of experiences to offer. Discover the true spirit of Santiago and its hospitable locals by visiting these hidden gems, which range from peaceful parks to obscure cathedrals, intimate cafes to cultural hubs. You'll find that the city's appeal goes far beyond its well-known attractions as you explore these hidden gems, leaving you with lifelong memories and a greater understanding of its rich history and culture.

Santiago de Compostela: A Cultural Odyssey - Festivals and Cultural Experiences

Nestled amid the verdant surroundings of Galicia, Spain, Santiago de Compostela is more than simply a city; it is a cultural tapestry, interwoven with vivid traditions, spirituality, and historical threads. This charming city offers a plethora of cultural events and festivals that take you back in time. It is well-known for being the Camino de Santiago pilgrimage's last destination. Through our exploration of Santiago de Compostela's bustling festivals and rich cultural heritage, we will delve into the city's heart and soul.

Encounters with Culture in Santiago de Compostela:

Journey to Santiago Cathedral (Catedral de Santiago): The cathedral, which is the last destination for pilgrims on the Camino de

Santiago and a UNESCO World Heritage Site, is the center of Santiago's culture. There's a strong sense of spirituality about the cathedral. It's a captivating experience to be at the Pilgrim's Mass and watch the enormous incense burner, or Botafumeiro, swing from the roof.

Wandering Through the Old Town (Casco Antiguo): The historic core of Santiago is a maze of streets made of cobblestones, quaint squares, and buildings dating back hundreds of years. Explore the little lanes, find secret courtyards, and take in this medieval city's breathtaking architecture.

Local Markets: Visit the Mercado de Abastos to fully experience the cuisine of the area. Galician specialties, such as handcrafted cheeses and wines and fresh seafood, are available for tasting here. Talk to amiable sellers to discover the authentic tastes of the area.

Galleries & Museums: Santiago is home to a wide range of cultural establishments that provide information about the city's past and present. The significance of the Camino de Santiago pilgrimage is explored at the Museo das Peregrinacións e de Santiago, while the city's art galleries feature both foreign and local talent.

Welcome to the Spanish custom of taking leisurely strolls through cafés. Enjoy a drink of Albariño wine or café con leche while sitting at a café in a picturesque plaza and observing the passing scenery. Santiago's café culture promotes sociability and relaxation.

Street performers & Live Music: Santiago's streets are frequently alive with the sounds of live music, particularly in the nights. Every music enthusiast will find something they enjoy, whether it's new genres or traditional Galician tunes. Buskers and street performers also contribute to the vibrant environment.

Libraries & Bookstores: Santiago's numerous bookshops and libraries honor the city's rich literary legacy. A magnificent antique library with elaborate woodwork and antiquated texts may be seen at the Colexio de San Xerome.

Santiago de Compostela Celebrations:

Celebrated on July 25th, the Feast of Saint James (Día do Apóstolo) is one of Santiago's most important holidays. Honoring Saint James, the patron saint of Spain, pilgrims from all over the world assemble in the city. Religious rites, processions, and an amazing fireworks show over the cathedral are all part of the festivities.

Carnival (Entroido): Held in February or March, Santiago's Carnival is a vibrant and energetic occasion. There are parades, music, and dancing in the streets, and people are dressed in extravagant costumes. It's a time to celebrate and have fun before the seriousness of Lent.

Holy Week (Semana Santa): Processions, religious gatherings, and the reenactment of biblical scenes characterize Semana Santa, which is the week before Easter. Santiago's traditions of Holy Week are rich in history and draw both residents and tourists.

Galicia commemorates its National Day (Día da Patria Galega) on July 25, which also happens to be the Feast of Saint James. Cultural activities, musical performances, and a strong sense of Galician patriotism are all part of the celebrations.

August marks the annual Festival of María Pita, also known as Festas de María Pita, which takes place in the neighboring city of A Coruña, not in Santiago. With parades, dancing, fireworks, and music, it's an amazing show. From Santiago, it's only a quick train ride to A Coruña.

The International Film Festival (Festival Internacional de Cinema Curtocircuíto) is a renowned film festival that aficionados should schedule their visit to attend around October. It serves as a gathering place for movie enthusiasts, showcasing a wide range of short films from around the globe.

Galician Folk Festivals: Santiago holds a number of folk festivals, or festas do pobo, all year long to honor Galician culture. These gatherings provide traditional cuisine, dancing, and music, letting you fully experience the way of life in the area.

Holiday Celebrations: Santiago de Compostela is especially charming in the winter. Festive lights and decorations fill the city, while Christmas markets appear in the squares. A calm and spiritual experience awaits you at the cathedral on Christmas Eve during the Midnight Mass.

The festivals and cultural events of Santiago de Compostela bear witness to the city's vivacious character and ingrained customs. Whether you're ready to immerse yourself in Galicia's rich culture or are walking the Camino de Santiago in search of spiritual enlightenment, this alluring city has a plethora of experiences that will make a lasting impression on your heart and soul.

Chapter 15

Souvenir Shopping in Santiago de Compostela: Unearth the Treasures of Galicia

Nestled in the heart of Galicia, Spain, Santiago de Compostela is a treasure trove for souvenir shopping in addition to being a place of spiritual pilgrimage. Numerous distinctive and regionally produced goods are available in this old city, making them wonderful mementos of your trip. We will go through the recommended goods to buy and the ideal spots to start your unforgettable Santiago de Compostela souvenir hunt in this comprehensive guide.

Section 1: Recommended Memorabilia

1.1 Vieira's Pilgrim's Shell:

The Camino de Santiago pilgrimage is represented by the scallop shell, or vieira in

Spanish. Vieiras come in a variety of shapes, sizes, and patterns; they are frequently worn as pendants or used as ornaments. Without a scallop shell, a pilgrimage isn't complete.

1.2 Certificates from Compostela:

A Compostela certificate is awarded to travellers who successfully complete the Camino de Santiago. Although you can get one for free, you can also find exquisitely made, personalized ones to treasure your travels.

1.3 Customary Crafts in Galicia:

Galicia is renowned for its handcrafted goods. Look for things like earthenware, pottery, and wooden crafts like intricately carved tambourines or walking sticks.

1.4 Wine Albariño:

The wine known as Albariño is a specialty of Galicia, namely from the Rías Baixas region. Get one or two bottles to enjoy the tastes of the area back home.

1.5 Textiles from Galicia:

Galicia is known for producing fine textiles, like as elaborate lacework, scarves, and traditional woolen blankets. These products provide stylish and comfortable keepsakes.

1.6 Customary Spanish Clothes:

If you have an eye for style, think about purchasing some traditional Spanish clothing, like a mantón de Manila (a beautiful silk shawl) or a flamenco dress.

1.7 Galician Culinary Treasures:

Acquire some local specialties, like as cheeses, canned fish, and pastries like tarta de Santiago (almond cake) or tetilla cheese, to take a piece of Galicia with you.

1.8 Chains:

Silver crosses, scallop shell pendants, and religiously related jewelry are among the one-of-a-kind items that can be found in Santiago's many jewelry boutiques, all of which are inspired by the Camino de Santiago.

Section 2: The Greatest Spots to Buy Souvenirs

2.1 Do Franco Road:

In the center of Santiago's Old Town, this busy street is a veritable gold mine of gift shops. Everything is available, including ceramics, fabrics, and scallop shells. Remember to take a look around the charming side streets that branch off of Rúa do Franco.

2.2 Abastos Market:

This bustling food market is a great spot to get culinary keepsakes from the area. Pick up some wine, cheeses, olive oils, and other gourmet treats to bring home.

2.3 La Acibechería Calle:

Calle de la Acibechería, also called the street of pilgrims' necessities, is lined with stores offering traditional Galician goods, such as textiles, holy symbols, and walking sticks carved by hand.

2.4 The Queixo House:

A large assortment of Galician cheeses may be found in Casa do Queixo, a cheese shop close to the Santiago Cathedral. It's an excellent location to buy and sample cheeses from the area.

2.5 Workshops for Ceramics:

Santiago is renowned for its ceramics, and you can see how these exquisite pieces are made and buy one-of-a-kind pottery by visiting neighborhood workshops like the Taller de Cerámica Pontejos.

2.6 Market at Alameda Park:

There's a weekly market at Alameda Park on Sundays where you may find a variety of jewelry, antiques, and crafts. It's a great place to peruse regional artisan goods.

2.7 Market of the Abastos Plaza:

Perfect for obtaining fresh, local vegetables and regional goods like honey, spices, and dried fruits, this market is situated close to the cathedral.

2.8 Shops on Camino de Santiago:

There are Camino de Santiago shops in Santiago, such as Camino Shop and Caminoteca, where you may buy a variety of pilgrim-related goods, such as apparel, souvenirs, and guidebooks.

Section 3: Buying Advice

3.1 Negotiation:

It's not typical to bargain at Spanish stores, especially not in well-established ones. You might be able to haggle a little bit over prices, though, at flea markets or with street vendors.

3.2 Duty-Free Purchasing:

On purchases over a specific value, non-residents of the European Union frequently qualify for a VAT refund. Seek out stores with the Tax-Free Shopping sign up and request the required paperwork.

3.3 Value for Class above Amount:

When shopping for mementos, spend more money on quality than quantity. Select objects that have special importance for you and that you will treasure as keepsakes of your journey.

3.4 Encourage Regional Artists:

Purchase directly from regional craftsmen or stores that procure their goods locally whenever at all possible. This guarantees that you are receiving genuine, handcrafted goods and boosts the local economy.

3.5 Verify Airport Rules:

Take note of airport policies restricting the carrying of liquids in your luggage if you are purchasing liquids such as wine or olive oil. Think about getting these products at the airport duty-free.

Section 4: Perspectives on Culture

4.1 Honor the Shell of the Scallop

In addition to being a memento, the scallop shell holds great symbolic value for the Camino de

Santiago journey. Show it respect and veneration.

4.2 Credentials of the Pilgrims:

You will start the Camino de Santiago with a pilgrim's certificate if you intend to walk it. Gather stamps, sometimes known as solos, as they are an essential component of the pilgrimage experience.

4.3 The Hospitality of Galicia:

Galicians are renowned for their friendly greetings. Engaging in dialogue with locals is highly recommended as they can provide insightful advice and recommendations.

In summary:

Purchasing souvenirs in Santiago de Compostela is a must-do activity for travelers who want to take a bit of Galicia's rich history and culture home with them. There are many of possibilities in the city, whether you're looking to buy locally created souvenirs, indulge in Galician cuisine, or gather scallop shells. Remember to enjoy the moment and acknowledge the individuality of every thing you come across as you peruse the city's markets and stores. Cheers to your shopping, and I hope your mementos become treasured keepsakes of this amazing place you visited!

Chapter 16

A 14-Day Exploration of Santiago de Compostela: A Comprehensive Itinerary.

With its fascinating history, deep spiritual significance, and lively culture, Santiago de Compostela is a city that begs visitors to experience its allure. You may fully explore the heart of this fascinating location with a 14-day vacation. With a two-week itinerary that covers everything from the famous Santiago Cathedral to the picturesque Galician landscapes, you can be sure to make the most of your time in this captivating Spanish city.

Day 1: Orientation and Arrival

Daybreak:

Reach the train station or Santiago de Compostela Airport.

Check into the lodging of your choice, ideally one that is in the heart of the city.

Start your adventure with a leisurely walk through the Old Town of Santiago, paying special attention to the beautiful architecture surrounding the Santiago Cathedral, or Praza do Obradoiro.

Afterwards:

Explore the interior of the Santiago Cathedral, including the crypt thought to contain Saint James's relics.

Visit the cathedral to attend the Pilgrim's Mass, which is typically held at midday (see the schedule).

Afternoon:

Visit a nearby restaurant and have a traditional Galician meal. Sample some local fare, such as empanadas and pulpo a la gallega (octopus).

Day 2: The Cultural Treasures of Santiago

Daybreak:

To learn more about the history of the Camino de Santiago, go to the Museo de las Peregrinaciones.
Investigate the Museo do Pobo Galego to learn more about Galician customs and culture.
Afterwards:

Explore the quaint Rúa do Franco and Rúa Nova, which are flanked with cafes, boutiques, and stores.
Visit the Centro Galego de Arte Contemporánea (CGAC) to learn about Santiago's artistic and historical heritage.
Afternoon:

In a nearby wine bar, savor tapas and wines from Galicia. Take in the lively ambiance of Santiago's nightlife.
Day 3: Meditation and Walking

Daybreak:

Walk some of the Camino de Santiago to begin your own pilgrimage. Spend a few hours walking a local route, like the Camino Francés or Camino Inglés.

See the Chapel of San Lázaro, where pilgrims are laid to rest.

Afterwards:

Go back to Santiago and ponder for a while at the Santiago Cathedral. Participate in a silent prayer service or light a candle.

Afternoon:

Have dinner in the Old Town and consider your journey thus far.

Day Four: Gardens and Parks

Daybreak:

Start your day in Alameda Park, where you may take in the expansive views of the city and its verdant surroundings.

Discover the tranquil grounds and artistic installations of Parque de Bonaval.

Afterwards:

Explore the tranquil surroundings and historic ruins of Parque da Rocha Forte.

Take a trip down the Río Sarela trail to experience the natural beauty of Santiago.

Afternoon:

Go back to the Old Town and eat in a restaurant that has outdoor seating or a garden.

Day 5: Full Day Visit to Muxía and Fisterra

All-Day Journey:

Take a day excursion to the seaside towns of Muxía and Fisterra (Finisterre), which are renowned for their breathtaking vistas of the Atlantic Ocean.

Discover the "End of the World" feeling that comes with exploring the lighthouse in Cabo Fisterra.

As the sun sets over the ocean, consider your adventure.

Day 6: History and Art

Daybreak:

Explore the Castro de Elviña, a historic Celtic hillfort boasting expansive vistas.

San Lorenzo de Trasouto is a quaint town that is worth exploring.

Afterwards:

Explore the Old Town's historic squares, streets, and hidden treasures during your visit.

Explore the ancient Casa de la Troya, which depicts traditional Galician living.

Afternoon:

Savor a typical Galician meal while listening to live folk music at a rustic pub.

Day 7: Tasting Adventures

Daybreak:

Visit the Mercado de Abastos, a lively market that serves fresh Galician products and delicacies, to start your day.

Meet local merchants and taste wines, cheeses, and seafood.

Afterwards:

Take a cooking lesson to learn how to make traditional Galician cuisine.
Enjoy your creations with local wines for lunch.
Afternoon:

To sample additional Galician dishes, such as lacón con grelos (pork with turnip greens), head to a nearby eatery.
Day 8: The Coast of Galicia

All-Day Journey:

Discover the charming beaches and fishing villages along Rías Baixas' gorgeous coastline.
Take a tour of the quaint town of Combarro, which is well-known for its waterfront traditional Galician horreos (granaries).
Savor a wine tasting experience in the Salnés Valley vineyards, renowned for their Albariño wine.
Day 9: Outdoor Sports and Adventure

Daybreak:

Enjoy the peace and quiet of the Galician countryside by giving kayaking a try on the Ulla River.
Alternatively, take a bike trip through the scenic bike routes of Santiago.
Afterwards:

Play a round of golf at the Real Aero Club de Santiago, which is tucked away in the beautiful Galician countryside.
Afternoon:

Either unwind at your lodging or experience Santiago's exciting nightlife.
Day 10: Retreat for Wellbeing

Whole Day:

Spend a rejuvenating and relaxing day at a Santiago spa or thermal bath facility.

Take advantage of a variety of services, such as massages and thermal pools, that are meant to help you relax and feel refreshed.

Day 11: The Dramatic Side of Santiago

Daybreak:

Visit Santiago's oldest and most prestigious theater, the Teatro Principal, first thing in the morning. To find out what concerts or guided tours are scheduled for your visit, check the schedule in advance. Experience the world of theater while admiring this iconic venue's stunning architecture.

Afterwards:

Visit the city's contemporary cultural complex, the Auditorio de Galicia, following your theater experience. Investigate the galleries, art installations, and exhibitions inside the auditorium. If you're planning to attend, see if any plays, concerts, or dance performances are scheduled. This venue frequently organizes a variety of cultural events. This is a great place to experience live music and become fully immersed in Santiago's cultural scene.

Afternoon:

Pick an Old Town restaurant for dinner that has an artistic or cultural vibe. Live music, flamenco presentations, and traditional dance performances are all featured in many restaurants. Indulge in a delectable lunch and watch the cultural show. For a truly Galician evening, make sure to try some regional cuisine and wines.

Day 12: Immersion in Language and Culture

Daybreak:

Become fully immersed in the culture of the area by signing up for a Spanish or Galician language course. All levels of language instruction are provided by a number of cultural organizations and language schools in Santiago. These lessons offer a special chance to engage with the community and obtain a better comprehension of the culture, regardless of your level of language proficiency.

Afterwards:

Engage in dialogue with locals to put your freshly gained language abilities to use. Go to a neighborhood café or plaza, have a coffee or a glass of Albariño wine, and strike up a conversation with the hospitable Santiago locals. This is a fantastic method to become familiar with their beliefs, customs, and way of life.

Afternoon:

Attending a course or cultural event will allow you to continue your language and cultural immersion. Seek out occasions such as folklore gatherings, storytelling events, or art exhibits. These encounters will strengthen your bond with Santiago's culture and leave you with priceless memories of your trip.

Day 13: Saying goodbye to Santiago

Daybreak:

On your last morning in Santiago, travel back to some of your favorite locations in the Old Town. Enjoy a final leisurely stroll along the old streets, taking in the quaint architecture and the atmosphere of the city.

Afterwards:

Have your farewell dinner at a nearby restaurant so you can taste Galicia's tastes one more time. Try some local sweets like Tarta de Santiago, which is an almond cake with Saint James' cross on top.

Afternoon:

Go to a viewpoint to catch a final look at Santiago de Compostela's skyline as the sun sets. Beautiful views of the city and its surroundings may be seen from the Monte Pedroso viewpoint. Think back on your travels and the experiences you've had in this amazing location.

Day 14: Leaving

Daybreak:

You might have some free time before your departure to pick up any last-minute gifts or mementos from Santiago. Look around markets, artisan stores, and boutiques in the area to find one-of-a-kind souvenirs of your trip.
Afterwards:

After leaving your lodging, head to the train or airport in Santiago de Compostela. Remember to come away from your 14-day journey in Santiago de Compostela with priceless memories, fresh insights, and a feeling of accomplishment.

A well-rounded view of Santiago de Compostela's rich history, cultural treasures, scenic beauty, and gastronomic delights is what this extensive 14-day itinerary aims to provide. It enables you to thoroughly experience the essence of this captivating city and depart with a profound understanding of its distinct charm and personality. Travelers of all stripes will find something to enjoy in Santiago de Compostela, whether they are pilgrims, culture vultures, nature lovers, or gourmets.

Essential Tips and Information for Travelers Visiting Santiago de Compostela.

The city of Santiago de Compostela is rich in spirituality, culture, and history. It is situated in northwest Spain. It draws visitors from all over the world as the Camino de Santiago pilgrimage's last endpoint. Planning ahead is crucial for a seamless and fulfilling trip to Santiago de Compostela, regardless of whether you're a pilgrim or a visitor. We'll give you all the advice and details you need to make the most of your trip to this fascinating city in this extensive guide.

Section 1: Travel Planning

1.1 The Ideal Time to Go:

Although you can visit Santiago any time of year, the ideal time to go will depend on your personal preferences. Enjoy nice weather and fewer crowds in the spring and early fall (April to June and September to October). Winter (December to February) can be cold and wet, and summers (July and August) can be very hot.

1.2 Length of Visit:

To fully enjoy Santiago's main attractions, allow yourself at least two or three days to spend there. Your route choice will determine how long it takes you to complete the Camino de Santiago trek.

1.3 Essentials of Packing:

Prior to your journey, check Santiago's weather prediction and make appropriate packing decisions. A power adaptor (Europe uses Type C and F plugs), rain clothing, suitable walking shoes, and a universal travel adapter are essentials.

1.4 Money and Modes of Payment:

The Euro (€) is the currency used in Santiago and Spain. Although most places take credit cards, it's a good idea to have extra cash on hand for smaller purchases. There are plenty of ATMs available for exchanging currencies.

1.5 Spoken Word:

The region's official language is Spanish, but Galician is also spoken there. Communication in Spanish can benefit from having a basic understanding of the language, even if many locals who work in the tourism sector speak English.

How to Get to Santiago de Compostela in Section Two

2.1 Aircraft:

Flights into and out of Santiago de Compostela Airport (SCQ) service the city. Make sure you have all the necessary travel paperwork, and if you want to get the best airfare, buy your tickets well in advance.

2.2 Railroad:

Train connections to Santiago are excellent, with fast trains operating from major towns such as

Madrid, Barcelona, and A Coruña. Situated in the heart of the city, the Santiago de Compostela Railway Station is easily accessible.

2.3 Van:

Another way to go to Santiago is by bus. The train station is close to the Estación de Autobuses de Santiago, which provides both local and international bus service.

A 2.4-car

Renting a car can provide you greater freedom if you're considering seeing more of northern Spain or Galicia. Make sure you have the appropriate insurance and driver's license for Spain.

Section 3: Place of Residence

3.1 Lodgings:

There are many different types of hotels in Santiago, ranging from opulent properties to affordable choices. Because of its close proximity to important sites, hotels are often found in the Old Town (Casco Antiguo).

3.2 Guesthouses and Homestays:

If you want a more authentic experience, think about booking a guesthouse or homestay. Numerous possibilities in Santiago are listed on websites such as Booking.com and Airbnb.

3.3 Holiday Homes:

For those who want more freedom and room, there are vacation rentals that include houses and apartments.

Hostels (3.4):

Hostels in Santiago are a great option for tourists on a tight budget, including pilgrims walking the Camino de Santiago.

Part 4: Getting Around Santiago de Compostela

4.1 Casco Antiguo, or Old Town:

It's better to explore Santiago's historic core on foot. It is a labyrinth of little squares, old buildings, and winding streets. Don't forget to check out the renowned Botafumeiro and Santiago Cathedral.

4.2 Transit by Public:

There is a bus system in Santiago that may transport you to different areas of the city. In order to enjoy unlimited bus and tram journeys throughout your visit, think about getting a Santiago Card.

Taxi (4.3):

Taxis are widely accessible and can be reserved in advance for longer trips or airport transfers, or they can be called on the street.

4.4% Cycling:

Thanks to designated bike lanes and bike-sharing programs, Santiago is becoming a more bike-friendly city. A fantastic method to get around the city is to rent a bike.

Section 5: Experiences with Dining and Cooking

5.1 Food from Galicia:

Don't miss sampling authentic Galician fare like octopus pulpo a la gallega, savory pies called empanadas, and pork with turnip greens called lacón con grelos. Go with a local Albariño wine to go with your dinner.

5.2 Gratuity:

In Spain, leaving a tip is traditional. Although a service charge is frequently included in the bill, it is customary to tip with little change or the entire amount rounded up.

5.3 Hours of Dining:

Dining hours in Spain are not like those in many other nations. Dinner usually starts at 8 p.m. or later, while lunch is normally served from 1 to 3 p.m.

Section 6: Health and Safety

6.1 Useful Phone Numbers:

In Spain, the emergency number for law enforcement, ambulance, and fire services is 112.

6.2 Medical Care:

Healthcare in Spain is of a high caliber. While non-EU visitors should have travel insurance that covers medical costs, citizens of the European Union may utilize the European Health Insurance Card (EHIC).

6.3 Safety Guidance:

Although Santiago is a relatively safe city for tourists, it's still a good idea to use common sense caution and keep an eye on your surroundings.

Section 7: Etiquette in Culture

7.1 Salutations:

Greetings usually involve a handshake. Two cheek kisses (from left to right) are the standard welcome in less formal situations.

Siesta 7.2:

Remember that a lot of stores and companies close from 2:00 pm to 5:00 pm for a siesta. Plan out what you're going to do.

7.3 Deference to Houses of Religion:

Respect ongoing religious ceremonies and dress modestly when visiting places of worship, such as the Santiago Cathedral.

The city of Santiago de Compostela combines spirituality, history, and cultural diversity. By adhering to the crucial advice and details in this guide, you'll be ready to discover its gems, enjoy its cuisine, and take in the distinctive ambience of this amazing location. Have fun traveling to Santiago de Compostela!

Made in United States
Troutdale, OR
02/10/2024

17552256R00166